D1546727

MAKING
EXHIBIT
LABELS

Beverly Serrell

A Step-by-Step Guide

American Association for State and Local History
Nashville, Tennessee

11163

Copyright © 1983 by the American Association for State and Local History. All rights reserved. Printed in the United States of America. Except for brief quotations used in critical articles or reviews, no part of this publication may be reproduced or transmitted in any form by any means, electronic or mechanical, including photocopying, re- cording, or any information storage/retrieval system, without written permission of the copyright owner. For more information, write to the American Association for State and Local History, 708 Berry Road, Nashville, Tennessee 37204.

Library of Congress Cataloging in Publication Data

Serrell, Beverly, 1943-
   Making exhibit labels.

   Bibliography: p.
   Includes index.
   1. Museum labels—Handbooks, manuals, etc. I. Title.
AM157.S47   1982   069.5   82-22614
ISBN 0-910050-64-3

All photographs were taken by the author except for Figures 1 and 3, which were taken by Tom Brennan, and Figure 2, courtesy of the Chicago Zoological Society.

The locations of the labels shown are not provided, since the photos serve only as generic examples illustrating discussion in the text.

Contents

Preface

Every museum has the responsibility of providing labels, and every visitor has the right to read them. This book seeks to make those experiences more rewarding for both parties. It is primarily directed to the people who write, edit, prepare, place, and evaluate labels, but it also aims to encourage other readers, museum staff and the public alike, to become advocates of good ones. *Making Exhibit Labels* focuses on the central goal of producing labels which museum-goers will read and understand. As a researcher in this field and also a generalist and inveterate visitor at museums, I have taken ideas and information from a variety of sources—on subjects ranging from museum philosophy to the nuts and adhesives of production.

Not long after deciding to write this book, I attended a meeting of local history museum professionals. I wanted to test the idea for the book, and at lunch I mentioned the subject to the director of a small, well-known historical society. When I asked what kind of information he would like to have in a book about museum labels, he replied, "The cheapest way to make them." His was not the response that I had hoped for, but it suggested the low priority which many museums give to labels and which is a perennial cause of labels' poor quality. Although this book does contain ideas for economical production, its main concern is with making the end result more interesting, readable, legible, and deserving of visitors' attention.

I hope that this book will help directors, curators, designers, and educators—or people who play more than one of these roles—to accomplish several objectives:

• to establish the necessary priority of labels and their importance as integral parts of exhibits;
• to elicit the support—particularly the time and money—necessary for the creation of good labels;
• to select the best processes for making labels;
• to set objectives when planning labels;
• to establish testable criteria for the effectiveness of labels;
• to swear by brevity, clarity, simplicity, legibility, and humanitarian concerns in label writing;
• to discourage counterproductive flights of fancy in label design, especially when they impair legibility;
• to reward good examples and to promote better ones.

The goal for readers of this book is not the achievement or expectation of perfection in museum

Preface

labels but the ability to recognize quality and to make intelligent decisions about it.

There are several people whose assistance and encouragement I found essential. I thank Nora Deans, Barbara Friedman, Gary Gore, and Ed Miller. Thanks also to Tom Brennan, Joan Cash, Betty Elder, Marcia Brubeck, Pete LaPaglia, Robert Lipman, Ross Loomis, Ed Lace, Jim Marlett, George Rabb, Bill Stribling, and Jim Sommer.

Making Exhibit Labels

1

Planning Labels for an Exhibit

Graphic communication delivers a message by means of words, symbols, art, photographs, and other visual images on a flat surface. We see familiar examples in books, newspapers, and magazines and on billboards, road signs, and food packages.

Museum labels are also a form of graphic communication. Their planning and preparation involves the same fundamental techniques—research, writing, design, layout, typography—used in other print media. Books and advertising are probably the most common forms of graphic communication, and museum labels rely heavily on them as resources and as models for appropriate techniques.

Although labels have much in common with other print media, they are unique in several respects. First, production involves more one-of-a-kind signs. When each label interprets a single specimen, each must be different. Second, museum signs involve great quantities of large type sizes. (Almost all museum labels need to use type larger than that found in books and magazines.) Both of these requirements present the writer and designer with special problems.

Newspapers, magazines, and advertising are ephemeral forms of graphic communication; it is anticipated that they will be read soon after production and will then be discarded. Books are much more permanent. As a consequence more time is devoted to the preparation of book manuscripts, and more money is spent on their printing. The results are expected to last for years. Museum labels, on the other hand, have small amounts of copy compared with books, yet people may expect them to last for years, often under adverse conditions.

Museum labels are also unique, unfortunately, in that although the number of people expected to read them is large, the amount of time spent on their preparation is often very brief and the amount of editing very little. With an annual attendance of 10,000 visitors, a museum exhibit on display for five years may draw at least 25,000 potential readers. A book prepared for such a market would undergo far more rigorous and numerous editing stages than the average exhibit label.

People do not visit museums primarily to read the labels, but this fact is no excuse for sloppiness on the part of

Table 1. A Comparison of Three Types of Graphic Communication

Type	Purpose	Words	Speed of writing and production	Type sizes	Longevity
Books	inform, entertain	thousands	months	mostly small	years
Advertisements	catch attention, sell	hundreds	weeks	large and small	weeks
Museum labels	inform, interpret	hundreds	days-months	mostly large	months-years

museums. Quality is important in labels, as it is elsewhere. No form of graphic communication should be prepared with the tacit assumption that it might *not* be worth reading.

Six Types of Labels

All museums use some form of labels. Nonexhibit labels are shown in figures 1, 2, and 3. They identify locations or give directions: Gift Shop, Gallery 1, Exit, or No Smoking. Other signs identify and interpret displays by providing titles, names, dates, stories, and captions. Exhibit labels deserve a classification of their own, grouped by their relative size, purpose, and number of words.

The types of exhibit labels have been discussed by various authors (see works by Fruitman and DuBro, Neal, and Wilson and Medina in the bibliography) and authors have used different terms. This list summarizes the main groups by purpose:

TYPE	PURPOSE
Title (main, headline)	to attract attention to inform about the theme to identify
Subhead (secondary)	to further identify or inform
Introductory (main, explanatory)	to introduce the themes to summarize the exhibit
Group (secondary)	to develop specific ideas related to a group of objects
Captions (specimen)	to interpret individual objects
ID (specimen identification)	to give basic facts, such as name, date, donor, etc.

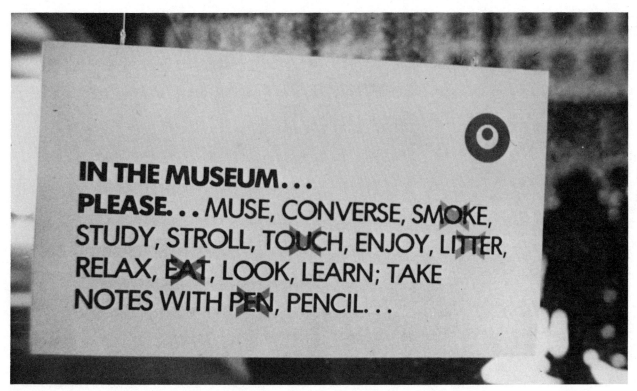

Figure 1. Sophisticated graphics on this nonexhibit sign make institutional rules seem less forbidding.

Figure 2. A nonexhibit sign giving directions.

Figure 3. When exhibit and nonexhibit signs appear together, the results are often whimsical.

Figure 4. Large, three-dimensional letters appear with a long introductory label.

One exhibit may not contain all the sorts of labels, and one label may fall into two categories. In any case different kinds should serve different purposes, and the distinctions should be readily apparent to the reader. This statement holds true regardless of the type of institution that is offering exhibits to the public. A history museum, a botanical garden, and a science center all use similar types of labels with similar purposes.

Every label needs a stated objective. Its purpose should be clearly decided before writing begins. Why is the label needed? What is it supposed to do? If these questions are not answered in the planning stage, confusion will follow— for the writer, for the editor, and ultimately for the visitor. The following section describes various types of labels and their functions.

Title labels identify the name of the exhibit. There should only be one title per exhibit, and it should be used consistently throughout the museum: the name should be the same on the floor plan, in the guidebook, and on the exhibit itself. (It is frustrating for visitors who are directed to Gallery X to find Exhibit Y never to be told when they had arrived.) Title labels usually contain fewer than ten words and frequently contain only one to five (see figure 4). Because they need to be prominent, they are usually the largest labels on exhibits. A title label should give enough information to enable visitors to decide whether they are interested in the subject matter, but it can also strive to arouse interest or curiosity.

Subhead labels announce the theme or clarify the title; an example is shown in figure 5. Subheads contain from one to ten or more words, depending on the complexity of the message. Different subheads may introduce different sections of an exhibit. Such labels should be large enough to permit visitors to read them from a distance while scanning the exhibit and deciding whether to look more closely. The subheads should make apparent the major messages of the exhibit.

Introductory labels serve to furnish the interested visitor with more details. The visitor who reads them will be interested, because by this time the title and the subheads will have weeded out people who are not interested. Introductory labels work best when they are placed near the beginning of the exhibit (see figure 6). They tend to be long, ranging from 50 to more than 200 words, set in large type, and they convey abstract messages—general concepts and ideas, overall views. They sketch the main themes and background and prepare the visitor to understand the specific information which will follow. There should only be one introductory label per exhibit or per subsection. The viewer who reads only the introductory

Figure 5. Title and subtitle (above display) introduce two opposing concepts, which are interpreted in the caption label (behind railing, center).

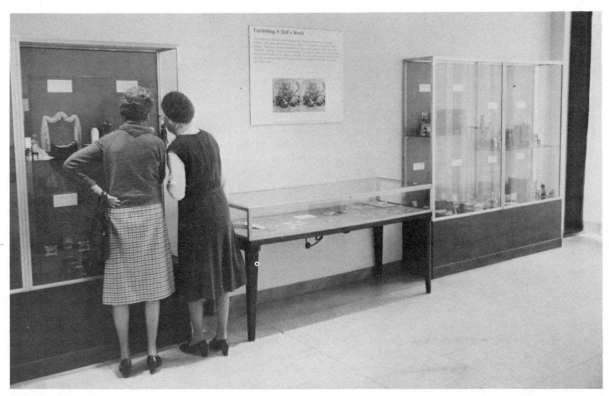

Figure 6. Placing the title and introductory labels together for temporary exhibits saves space and money.

Figure 7. A group label interprets the objects collectively.

label should grasp the major concepts and the exhibit's reason for being.

Group labels focus on similar objects. They interpret the likenesses apparent in the collection—similarities of function, form, or properties, as figure 7 suggests. Group labels interpret several objects collectively and may be long—more than 100 words—or short. Such signs should give the viewer a feeling for some of the unique characteristics of the objects shown; the reader should learn the exhibit themes and should acquire more background information necessary to understand the captions for individual specimens.

Captions, illustrated in figures 8 and 9, interpret single artifacts. They accompany individual objects and differ from specimen identifications in being longer and more complete. They contain from 10 to 100 words, full sentences, and very concrete and specific information. It is not necessary or even desirable for captions to be of uniform length, because some artifacts require more copy than others. Captions are usually fairly small in size. To read them the visitor must stand close to them and must be interested in specific details about the particular object described. Captions may point out features to observe and compare, may raise questions that can be answered by observation, and may relate objects to the general themes of the exhibit. In participatory exhibits, captions give directions for use of the exhibit.

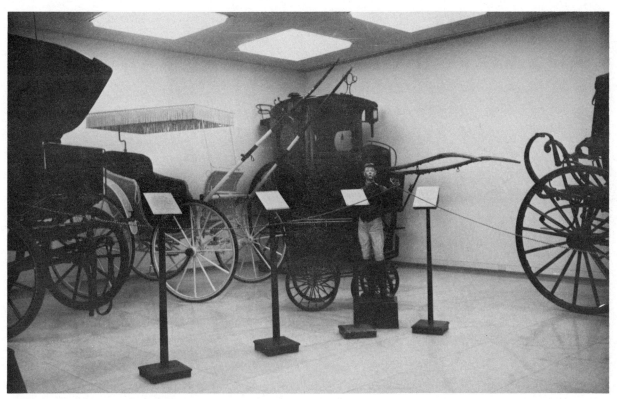

Figure 8. Captions located on free-standing stanchions interpret individual pieces in the collection.

RIDING THE CIRCUIT, 1849-60
In Lincoln's day, lawyers "rode the circuit", going from one county seat to another to attend Court. Here we see Lincoln, the attorney, arriving at the Court House square, Metamora, Woodford County, Illinois, for the semi-annual session of the Circuit Court, 8th judicial district. Lincoln is conversing with friends and clients. Court week was a gala affair and people from the surrounding countryside came to town for their semi-annual purchase of supplies.

Figure 9. Captions refer to specifics, as in "Here we see" in this miniature diorama.

ID, or specimen identification, labels are shown in figures 10 and 11. They contain the facts necessary for technically distinguishing one object from all others. Often only the name, date, origin, catalog number, donor, and scientific name appear. IDs are small, with few words, in an outline format. They need not be concerned with themes, with interpretation, or with motivating visitors. They present only the minimum facts.

Exhibits should be planned to contain several different types of labels used in a consistent manner. Labels need not conform to the kinds described here, but each should have a recognizable function and should be clearly presented. Avoid mistakes such as:

• burying main messages in specimen IDs;
• allowing abstract concepts to dominate captions;
• omitting titles or giving them only in the brochure.

Each label's function should be specified *before* the label is written, for the objective should guide the writing process. Each label's job links it with others in the same exhibit.The labels should complement one another, without competing for the reader's attention or distracting from the objects displayed.

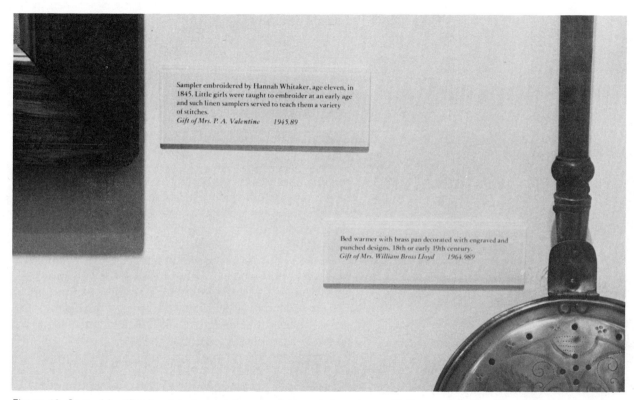

Sampler embroidered by Hannah Whitaker, age eleven, in 1845. Little girls were taught to embroider at an early age and such linen samplers served to teach them a variety of stitches.
Gift of Mrs. P. A. Valentine   1945.89

Bed warmer with brass pan decorated with engraved and punched designs, 18th or early 19th century.
Gift of Mrs. William Bross Lloyd   1964.989

Figure 10. Some identification labels contain some interpretation along with the usual facts—title, date, donor, and acquisition number.

13

Figure 11. Art museums often refrain from interpreting and provide labels that merely identify.

Interpretation

"Interpretation" has traditionally been oral, and the term is often used to describe the talks and demonstrations given by park naturalists for visitors to outdoor recreation centers. Extensive experience has shown that interpretation is most successful when guides focus on what visitors can see, feel, and understand in terms of their own experience. Interactions between the interpreter and the visitor elicit questions and suggest the group's areas of greatest interest as well as immediately alerting the interpreter when the audience becomes bored or confused. Interpretation involves the interaction of information, ideas, objects, and people, with an emphasis on participation and comprehension. Interpretation is not a matter of lecturing to a passive audience.

Museum staff regard interpretation as central in museum education, and labeling—even though human interaction is lost—is one way to accomplish it. Interpretive labels are easy to spot, as in the following example from Gail Casterline's *Archives and Manuscripts*. Which of these labels for an archival piece is interpretive?

• Letter from Congressman John Armstrong to his wife, 1900.

• Armstrong's 1900 campaign drew angry protests from woman suffrage advocates, as related in this letter to his wife.

The second label arouses curiosity and encourages the reader to explore the artifact (in this case, the letter itself) closely.

Museums have their own history of oral interpretation, but it differs significantly from that of parks and other recreation facilities. At one time museums were interpreted orally by their curators for the benefit of other collectors and specialists. The curator's interpretation tended to assume specialized knowledge, since lay people did not visit the museum. In fact, there was resistance to the idea of allowing the public into the museum at all. When museums did open their doors to the public—and when professional staff consequently retreated behind the scenes—labels took on the role of interpretation, but in language often still addressed to the expert. Even today, many labels in museums clearly belong in the tradition of "curator's talk," despite early and eloquent instructions from F. A. Lucas and F. J. North (see the bibliography), both curators themselves, who recognized the potentially educational and interpretive role for museum labels and saw a need for greater restraint.

The Planning Process

Exhibit labels are not read in isolation. They are part of the exhibit as a whole, and it is difficult to consider them without remembering their context. During planning, labels created for *new* exhibits are subject to constraints different from those affecting labels newly prepared for old or *existing* exhibits.

New exhibits offer the chance to start with a story, or with one central theme, around which ideas can be developed. Objects selected to illustrate the ideas are grouped logically. Different levels of labels can be planned—from titles and subheads to IDs—with each kind playing a different role and carrying the story along. Labels of different sizes can be designed to relate to each other in an integral way.

With old exhibits, you are often stuck with an incomplete or a fragmented story—sometimes no story at all—and new labels must impose some logic on the display. If there are no clear themes, it may be impossible to write subheadings or group labels. Individual captions may therefore become very important for old exhibits. When captions are the only labels, however, considerable restraint must be used, and very limited objectives must be set, for many long captions will tire even the most dedicated readers, will spoil the visual design, and will defeat their own purpose. If the captions constantly threaten to become 200 words long, try placing some of the information in leaflets, or in a brochure, instead.

Whether you are planning one label or a set of new labels for an old display or for a whole new exhibit, many different factors must be weighed and balanced. The question "How should I make the letters?" is as important as "How many words should I use to say it?" and "What can I use for materials so the visitors won't peel it off in a week?" Money and time will influence your priorities, and your compromises should result in the best solutions for your situation. The trick is to think through all questions before spending any money, thereby avoiding expensive mistakes.

Start by deciding what kind of labels you want to write and what their functions should be. What should the labels do?

Setting Objectives

In some cases a label may serve only to identify. In other cases the label will serve to interpret. Setting objectives means identifying the purpose and the intended audience for each label. There are two different philosophies with respect to audiences.

1. The "we won't stoop to the lowest common denominator" attitude says that labels should be written by specialists in the subject matter, for visitors who have some prior knowledge, who can appreciate the additional information, and who want to take the time to read.

2. The "serve the broadest possible audience" attitude suggests that labels should be written by someone skilled in communication, for visitors who are motivated to read but have very little prior knowledge and not much time to spend.

The first approach limits the number of readers who will be able to understand the label to those who have a certain prior knowledge of the subject. This attitude also suggests that if a visitor cannot comprehend the label, the visitor is at fault. In public institutions which claim to have an educational purpose and are supported by federal, local, and private grants and/or by taxes, this elitist stance is inexcusable.

The second approach presupposes that labels can appeal to people with prior knowledge and can also be understood by those without it who are interested in the subject. If the label is to do more than identify, then it should be made with a broad audience in mind.

By setting and striving to meet objectives, you will make the point of the label clearer to the reader. A label with seventeen facts in sixty-eight words has no objectives; writers who explain that "we just want readers to get whatever they can" are simply attempting to excuse pointless labels. Objectives are necessary if the label is to serve a purpose.

Scheduling

Once you have set objectives you will want to consider design, content, fabrication, and placement.

Design checklist
  Size
  Typeface
  Color
  Layout
  Illustrations

Design considers the overall appearance of the label. Size often must be considered first. Given the amount of space you have for the exhibit, and the space needed for the objects, how much room remains? Do you want a lot of signs, or do you prefer to downplay the written word? Once you have decided how large the labels might be, consider what size of type will be used, taking into account the readers' distance from it. How many words in that size of type will fit on the sign? Good design, color, and graphics can enhance good words but cannot substitute for them.

Content checklist
  Concepts
  Number of words
  Language and style
  Reading level

Content questions are several. What do you want to say? How do you want to say it? What resources are available? How much time do you have for research? Content is selected with the audience in mind. Who will be reading it? Who is it meant for? How much can you assume that readers already know? What can you say that will involve the reader with the exhibit? How can you make the labels more readable?

Content must be balanced appropriately with design. If you have more to say than space allows, either the content must be trimmed or more room must be found. Using a smaller size of type to squeeze copy into a small area is not a good solution.

Fabrication checklist
  Materials
  In house or contract out
  Deadlines

Fabrication means deciding on the materials that will be used to make the signs and deciding who will do the work. What methods do you use now? How long do they take? Are you satisfied with them? Are you looking for ways to improve the quality of production? Will it be done by you or contracted out? How soon do you need the finished product?

AA15046 3/8/83 AASLH $10.45

Placement checklist
  Mounting
  Fasteners
  Lighting
  Viewing angles
  Removal

Placement needs to be considered from the beginning to avoid reflective glare, neck strain, or too-easy removal. The placement of labels should also take into consideration the growing numbers of older visitors and people who wear bifocals.

The appendix lists materials for permanent and temporary installation methods.

Another way to plan at the outset is to set up a label production schedule. Given your own conditions and resources, begin by listing all the major label-related jobs and assigning them to the person most suited to carry them out, indicating when they should be done (you might use a planning form like that shown in table 2).

For an expanded production schedule, including all aspects of exhibitions, see *Good Show!* by Lothar Witteborg.

What Is an Effective Label?

Different people have different views, depending on their own perspectives, which often ignore a comprehensive definition. To a designer, an effective label might be one that is artistically pleasing, professionally silk-screened, or in harmony with the exhibit design. To an editor, the ideal will be well written and devoid of superfluous words or spelling errors. To an educator, an effective label might contain the appropriate message for a tour's theme. Each is right, but more is involved.

The best labels do what they are supposed to do in terms of their purpose, their intended audience, and their design. To be truly effective, they must succeed at all three levels. A good label conveys the intended message to the intended audience. It is readable, legible, and captures attention—and most important, is read.

The expected readership for labels will vary with the nature of the object and/or the kind of exhibit or display. Very popular, intrinsically interesting exhibits will attract more readers than out-of-the-way or less dramatic objects. Readership should be estimated accordingly. Well-written, appropriately placed, legible labels on popular exhibits can be expected to attract the attention of as many as 80 percent of the viewers who stop at the exhibit. Changes in design, content, methods of preparation, and placement that seek to make labels more effective can be judged successful if they lead to more readership.

Eight Deadly Sins

Effective labels do not happen by chance. They result when people know what to do and do it, whether the

Table 2. A Label Production Schedule

	Who	When
Set label objectives		
Research content		
Write		
Edit		
Test for effectiveness		
Design		
Produce		
Install		

museum staff consists of one or one hundred. If labels are not effective, the problem may lie at any number of different levels. The complaints and excuses are the same at museums all over the country. "We don't ever seem to get around to it"; "I'm waiting for a grant"; "It's his job, but he doesn't do it"; "She writes too much and won't let anybody edit it"; "He writes labels for other curators, not for visitors"; "She is a prima donna"; "He is a prima donna"; "We put them up but the visitors don't read them"; "The director doesn't believe in having labels."

The results of such problems are: (1) there are no labels, or (2) the existing labels are not effective.

Unsuccessful labels (see figures 12 and 13) suffer from one or more eight deadly sins. They may be:

1. too long and wordy;
2. too technical for the intended readers;
3. boring, with inappropriate information;
4. badly edited, with mistakes in grammar, spelling, or syntax;
5. too small—tiny words crammed on a 3 × 5 card;
6. hard to read (the result of poor typography);
7. colored in a way that makes reading difficult or tiresome;
8. badly placed, causing neck, back, or eye strain in the viewer.

These sins fall roughly into three main categories: writing, editing, and typographical design. Each is the subject of a later section.

The Average Visitor
Labels should address the average visitor. Data describing this person can be obtained by surveys—through questionnaires, interviews, or observations of people's behavior. In the absence of survey data, the characteristics of the average visitor can be obtained by thinking about the audience as clearly and objectively as possible and by comparing notes with others who know the museum well. From such information, a list of the typical features of the

musem's visitors can be generated. Actual survey data, in many cases, will merely confirm hunches researched by careful thinking.

The average visitor, although referred to in the singular, represents a plurality—the people who would occupy the central area of a bell curve describing the number of visitors in the audience with certain characteristics in common, such as age level, sex, group type (family, peers, school), group size, place of residence, income level, education background, and reason for visiting.

The average visitor at one museum may be quite different from the average visitor at another. For example, a suburban zoo might have more family groups, and larger groups, than a downtown art museum. Each museum should form an accurate picture of the predominating characteristics of the people it serves.

Even though individual audiences may vary, certain assumptions can be made about the average visitor (excluding students on tours) to almost any museum. Such a person will be

1. an adult able to read;
2. a reader of labels if they seem interesting;
3. pleasant, uncomplaining, and appreciative;
4. not very knowledgeable about the subject matter but curious and motivated to learn;

Figure 12. A 600-word label is considered too long for most animal captions in American zoos.

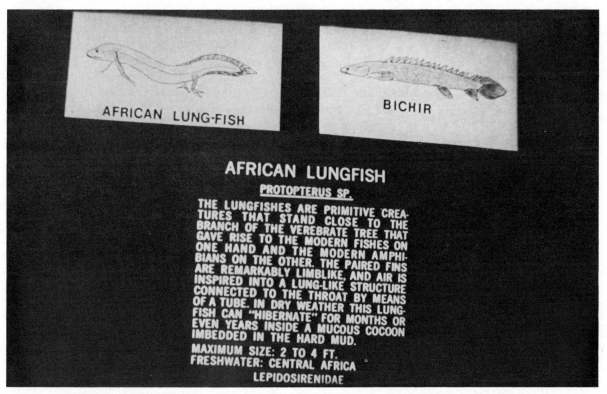

Figure 13. Poor typographical design hinders reading. All capital letters and large gaps between words create rivers of space running down the label. Note that the word "lungfish" appears both with and without a hyphen.

5. a lazy reader who will not bother with a label that is very long or difficult to read;
6. five feet six inches tall, someone who may not wear glasses but probably does not have perfect vision;
7. usually accompanied by someone who is personally close (people tend to share their museum experiences).

If you write with these characteristics in mind, your labels will be more appealing and appreciated. Make the law of averages work in your favor by not striving in vain to write for everyone.

When Not to Use Labels

All museums need identification and direction labels so that visitors can find their way about the museum and know what they are looking at. The most controversial type of sign is the interpretive label, and there has been much debate as to whether interpretation is appropriate for some exhibits. Museums may choose not to interpret their exhibits through labeling but may provide some other form of interpretation such as a guidebook, audio device, or docent tour. Figure 14 shows one example.

Art museums have the longest history of controversy about interpretive labels. It has been argued that an artist's creation should be approached by each individual alone, that a label should not force one interpretation on the viewer. Other people say that labels lack the space to do justice to all the possible different interpretations and therefore cannot offer a balanced view. In many cases, the original artist's meaning (if there was one) has not been recorded, and the museum may not want to take sides if different art historians have conflicting opinions. In other cases an artist may wish the work to be seen as nearly as possible without any preconceptions—without even an identification label—to discourage interpretation by association. If the purpose of the display is to invite every visitor to find personal meaning in the objects, then do not use labels. Without interpretation, however, fewer visitors will probably be able to relate the object to their own experience.

Children's museums and children's zoos do not lend themselves to interpretive labeling, yet interpretation will very likely occur in these settings by other means, perhaps through parent-child interactions, participatory exhibits, demonstrations, or docent help. Where clear alternatives are provided, labels may be superfluous. Successful interpretation by other means may make labels unnecessary. Then, too, a few exhibits "say it all" without words. No verbal means of interpretation—either spoken or written—is needed when the message is purely visual, as it would be, for example, in a display intended to communicate an undiluted feeling of beauty, mystery, inspiration, or even

Figure 14. An on-site interpreter can eliminate the need for labeling.

tragedy. (Purely visual messages are sometimes enhanced with music.) It is a good idea, however, to evaluate non-verbal exhibits to ascertain that the message *is* being communicated effectively without words. You may need to add a label as an afterthought if viewers are missing or are misinterpreting an important point.

2
Writing Copy

Making labels, from conception to production, requires expertise in several different specialties: researching, writing, editing, typography, and design. In some museums, the expertise may be concentrated in one person; in others, the jobs may be distributed among two or more individuals or departments. Each step in the creative process calls for special skills and tools.

Caption labels require more creative skill of the writer than do most other types. The caption is probably the most underused form of interpretation and the most abused—it often falls victim to one or more of the eight deadly sins. It will therefore receive much attention in this section on writing, with many examples.

Although there are many different kinds of museums, with varied philosophies and collections, effective museum labels have much in common, regardless of the setting. Good caption labels have two major characteristics:

1. They assume little prior knowledge on the part of the visitor.
2. They deal with immediate information—that which the visitor can experience firsthand.

The Necessary Tools

The tools of the *writer* include books, journals, consultants (such as librarians and subject-matter experts), pens and paper, dictionary and thesaurus, telephone (to call for help), and good examples to use for guidance and inspiration. The writer must have a strong and positive interest in the topic and a good nose for ferreting out information. Writers who are experts in the field about which they are writing have some advantages; for example, they may have to spend little time researching. On the other hand, lay people may find it easier to keep to the basics and may write less technically and more appealingly for the average visitor.

The tools of the *editor* are a dictionary, a manual of style, a red pen, and scissors and tape for cutting and rearranging copy. The editor must have a strong sense of sympathy and concern for the readers' comfort. Editors should also have a good ear for the sound of copy.

The tools of the label *designer* are standard rulers and pica sticks (showing typographers' measures), a book on architectural standards, typographical standards, artistic talent (or access to it), and an eye for legibility and aesthetically pleasing qualities.

Researching the Subject

From the beginning, do not lose sight of the objects and objectives you are writing about—keep them literally in your sight by taping pictures of them to a nearby wall. The pictures will prevent you from wandering into lengthy abstractions. Visitors come to museums to see the objects, so make your labels help them see more. In your research, collect information that enhances the ways of looking at things.

Sources of information can be found in print, in audio-visual resources, and in people—both the experts and the visitors themselves. When you are researching label copy for new exhibits or for objects already on exhibit, visitors are a very reliable source of ideas and inspiration. Casual, unobtrusive observations of visitors can yield new insights. Listen to the things they say. What kinds of questions do they ask? What do they want to know? What kinds of misunderstandings do you hear?

Listening gives you information quite different from that which you might elicit by asking questions. Visitors tend to say what they think you want to hear, or they will try to impress you with how much they already know. They will often inflate their interest in the subject or will exaggerate their motivation to learn. It *is* useful to ask visitors what they like or what they want, but you must balance their replies with their actual behavior as you observe it. For example, visitors may say that they are fascinated by Inca pottery but may spend an average of only five seconds in front of the case. Be aware also that people may claim more interest in abstract ideas but will comprehend and remember the more simple and concrete concepts (see *What's in a Name?* by Minda Borun and Maryanne Miller).

You can also gather valuable information by talking to experts outside the museum. Often they are flattered to have the opportunity to tell you what they know and think. Even if they seem unwilling at first, you may find it difficult to stop them in the end. Use a tape recorder when interviewing, and transcribe the tape later. You will be rewarded with the thoroughness of this method, even though it takes extra time.

Researching printed matter in libraries has been made easier in the last few years by improved technology. Computer searches can reveal subjects and titles in seconds; some manual searches used to take days. In addition, resources are often shared in interlibrary loan programs. If you are a member of one library, few doors to others are closed. "Infopass" provides members of one institution with access to others for specific research.

Records and Notes

As you research, take notes and jot down ideas as they come to you. Do not try to follow too rigid a structure at first. Record everything that you think might be useful. Save everything. Keep accurate and complete citations of references and other sources, and date all your notes. Material not used for labels may be useful for a guidebook, for other subsequent publications, for audiovisual scripts, or for education programs.

Gather far more information than you expect to use. When it comes time to write, you will be able to pick and choose as seems best for each label. Some facts are better for general signs, such as introductory or group labels. Others are better for captions or IDs. Material that may seem trivial can be included during the research phase and can be deleted later if it does not prove useful.

Once you have assembled your notes, you must condense and clarify your information to make concise, interesting, readable copy. Before attempting to do so, refer back to your objectives, review the themes and types of labels you plan to use (their purpose and size), and then form an image of the finished product in your mind. One source for such an image is *National Geographic*.

A Model to Study

National Geographic can suggest ideas about the amount of copy, style, level of language, and design. Look at one of their articles and think of it as an exhibit: the objects displayed are the photographs, and the copy represents the various kinds of labels. There is a title and maybe a subhead. The photograph captions—or legends, as they call them—interpret the photos. The author and photo credit lines are the ID labels. The story—the main body of the article—represents the museum catalog: it is only for people who are really interested in the subject. Most people just look at the photos and read the captions. The magazine writers know this and design their articles to accommodate the average reader.

The first one to five words of the legends are in bold type—darker letters, in contrast to the rest of the legend copy. These words are meant to catch the reader's attention. Very often the boldface highlights colorful, active language, and the legend style is rich with alliterations and metaphors. The legends as a group provide the gist of the article, and the first few lines contain enough of the story to put the point across. The remainder provides additional concepts, ideas, or facts.

Some legends are short—only one line, with fewer than 25 words. Many others range from 50 to 80 words, and a few are more than 200 words long. The variety of lengths adds interest to the copy and to the layout.

While the legends can stand on their own, that is, tell the story by themselves without the photos or the text of the article, they still play a role appropriately secondary to that of the photos. The labels do not upstage the "objects." Another point to notice is that the legends always begin by referring to something plainly visible in the photograph.

Furthermore, although they start with a concrete reference to what the reader can see, they are rarely redundant, nor do they state the obvious. The techniques allow the readers/viewers to make their own discoveries, including those of a nonverbal nature.

Legends in *National Geographic* are widely read because they are carefully researched, well written, and appropriate for the audience. Their quality is not surprising, given a special staff prepares them. The legend writers work according to a set of very specific guidelines, yet within the guidelines there is plenty of room for variety. The results are effective and worthy of imitation by museum label makers.

Sitting Down to Write

To write well, you must be in the mood. Do not force yourself to write a label when you are not ready. If it is your job to write labels, however, the sooner you are ready the better. The office, with its distractions, may be the worst place in which to write creatively. Wait until you have some time uninterrupted and alone: no phone calls, no tight schedule. You should be relaxed, and a glass of wine is not a bad idea, although it might be frowned on at the office. Set up the ideal conditions for your own writing mood.

Regardless of when you do the actual writing, be alert to your creativity at unexpected, unplanned moments—while you are driving to work or are in the shower. You will find that if you have done your homework—if you have clearly specified your ideas and objectives and have researched the subject matter thoroughly—inspirations may come upon you at almost any time. Capture those moments. Carry a small tape recorder with you or have the package of 3 × 5 index cards handy so you can record the message when it occurs to you instead of struggling to remember it hours later. Even your dreams may be a source of ideas—learn to remember them, too.

The First Draft

When you have pen in hand, or sit at the typewriter, the time has come.

1. Imagine yourself in the setting where the label will be.
2. Picture the object or objects (or look at a picture).
3. Picture the average visitor encountering the label.
4. Glance over your research notes.
5. Make a brief outline.
6. Begin to write.

At this point it is not important to worry about spelling, grammar, or syntax. Do not worry about getting the label right; just get it written. Write more than is called for—editing comes later. Try now simply to set down ideas and information that flows from one concept to the next.

Techniques for Adding Human Interest

Two ingredients of good nonfiction writing should be human interest and warmth, but many labels are cold, distant, and encyclopedic. There are several techniques for making labels more interesting, and most of them mean engaging the reader in an active, rather than passive, role by the use of:

- Questions. Stimulate the reader's imagination and curiosity. Questions work well at the beginning or in the body of the copy. Avoid asking "Why . . . ," however, unless you plan to give the answer immediately. Such questions are usually too abstract; still, they can often be reworded so that they stimulate people to look and to think.
- Colloquial expressions. The average visitor feels much more comfortable with familiar language than with technical or scientific jargon (see figure 15).
- Quotations. They can lend a human and appealing touch, as in figure 16.
- Comparisons. Relate aspects of one object to another, choosing something that is sure to be familiar to most people.
- Experience. Museum visitors probably go to other institutions or sites and probably watch TV. Make references to common experience when appropriate. See figure 17.
- Instructions. Occasionally ask or tell visitors what to look for; figure 18 provides a good example. Give hints on what to find, compare, or question in the exhibit. A label can invite the reader to interact instead of being a cold list of facts processed by a computer data system.
- Interesting titles. Capture visitors' attention and interest with a title that invites them to read on.
- Parody. Used with discretion, this form of humor is quite effective. Literature, poetry, and even advertisements are fair game for imitation.

Three Elements of Good Style

In addition to these techniques for adding warmth, there are three important ways of making labels more interesting, attractive, and easy to read:

1. Begin with the visual, observable interpretations and facts about the objects.
2. Use active verbs, and avoid the verb "to be."
3. Keep sentences under twenty-five words long. Vary the length, but keep an average of fifteen words per sentence.

Although these are not hard and fast rules, they should be treated as firm guidelines. You should think twice before deviating from them, and you should be able to say what your reasons are for doing so. Each of the three rules calls for some elaboration.

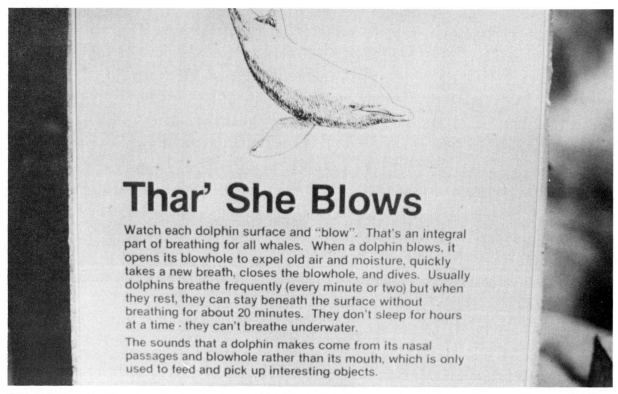

Thar' She Blows

Watch each dolphin surface and "blow". That's an integral part of breathing for all whales. When a dolphin blows, it opens its blowhole to expel old air and moisture, quickly takes a new breath, closes the blowhole, and dives. Usually dolphins breathe frequently (every minute or two) but when they rest, they can stay beneath the surface without breathing for about 20 minutes. They don't sleep for hours at a time · they can't breathe underwater.

The sounds that a dolphin makes come from its nasal passages and blowhole rather than its mouth, which is only used to feed and pick up interesting objects.

Figure 15. Catchy title, interesting content, and attractive, legible design make this label effective. (Some stylistic irregularities might distract the reader, however, and a good editor would catch them.)

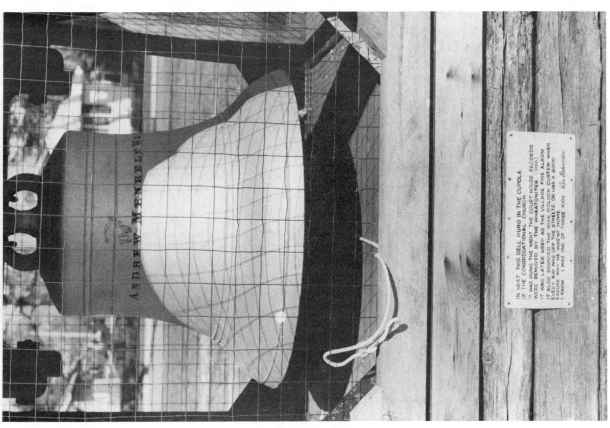

ANDREW MENEELY

IN 1847 THIS BELL HUNG IN THE CUPOLA
OF THE CONGREGATIONAL CHURCH.
IT WAS RUNG THE NIGHT THE COURT HOUSE RECORDS
WERE REMOVED BY THE WHEATONITES (1861)
IT WAS LATER USED AS THE VILLAGE FIRE ALARM.
IT ALSO SOUNDED THE NINE O'CLOCK CURFEW WHEN
EVERY KID WAS OFF THE STREETS OR HAD A GOOD
EXCUSE WHY HE WASN'T HOME.
I KNOW — I WAS ONE OF THOSE KIDS

Figure 16. Quotations add warmth and human interest to information.

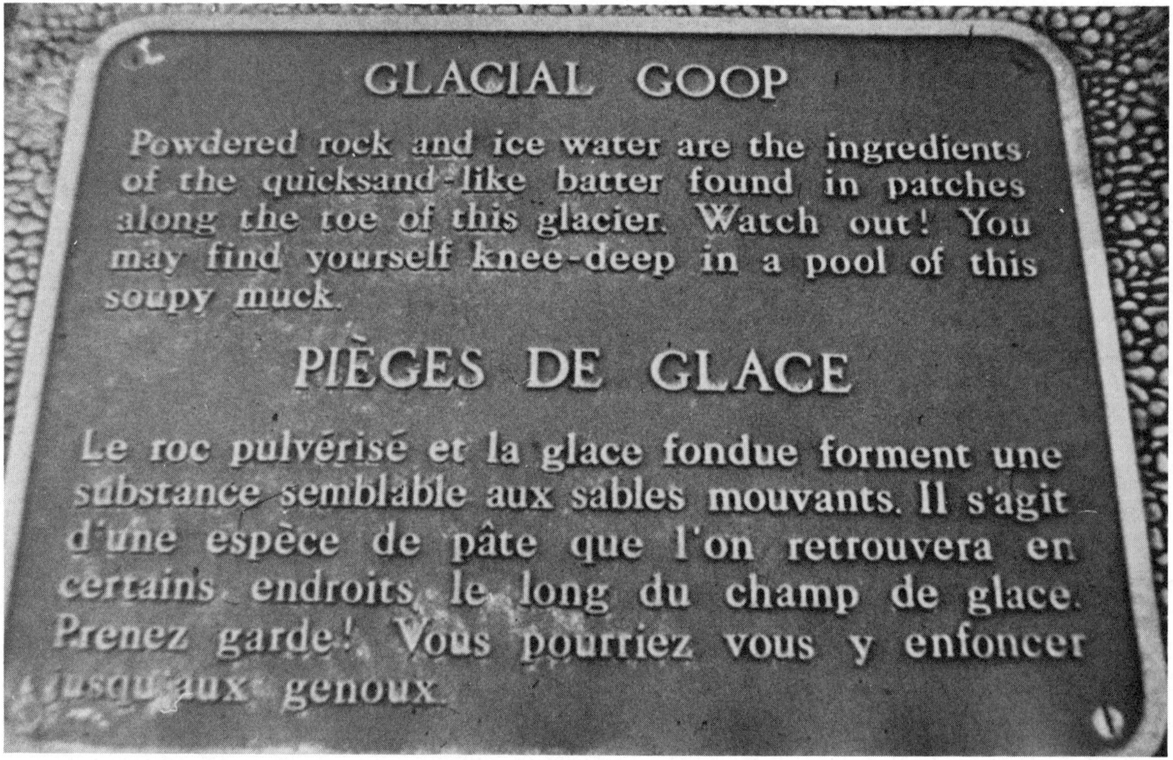

Figure 17. The warning on this bilingual label for Canadian audiences came too late for some readers, who stepped in the goop before seeing the sign.

The museum setting holds a vast potential for learning characterized by active, firsthand experiences and well-defined ideas. Topics which can be used to stress informal learning through observable information and interpretation include:

- Shape, sizes, and other physical properties. An example from a caption for a plate painted with abstract designs:

  The main motif in the center of the plate shows a Chinese-style lotus scroll. Floral sprays curl around the inside, and a wave-and-rock pattern fills the flattened rim.

- Origin or use:

  Fired at reveille and retreat, the cast iron signal gun also announced official gatherings such as treaty negotiations.

  To make horsehair, once common as a furniture covering, weavers used a warp of black linen yarn and a weft of hair from the tails of horses, oxen, cows or pigs.

- The ways in which the museum cares for the object or objects.
- The significance of the name.
- The distinctions between objects in a group. An example from a portion of a caption for a scroll painting at an art museum for a sophisticated audience:

The representation of melodramatic emotion characterizes the art of the Kamakura period. In contrast to the decorous display of grief in the earlier work, mourners here writhe on the ground in flamboyant agony.

The language used here is not simple, but it is extremely colorful and precise.

Give your viewers specifics to look for, and point out things they might otherwise miss. If the objects are alive, consider mentioning frequent behaviors that may be observed.

Begin labels with the specific and concrete, and then move on to general or abstract thoughts. Because visitors are diverse, the way to make sure you appeal to what they have in common is to speak to what they can see and experience—in an immediate sense. In short, if you can see it, write about it. Topics which tend to be more abstract and less visual include: history, relationships with other things not on exhibit, taxonomy, geographical distribution (a map can make this more concrete), future projections, and subjective feelings, such as honesty or value.

Probably the single characteristic that most often makes museum labels boring is their lack of active verbs. The result is flat and dull. Example: "This is the bed used by George Washington for sleeping." "George Washington slept here" is so much more memorable!

The CAMP COMMISSARY sold nothing but essentials, mainly work clothes and tobacco. A logger's clothes were his trademark. Specialized and adapted to his work, the logger needed clothes that were functional and provided freedom of movement. Pants were cut off or "stagged" below the boot tops to keep the rain out and to prevent snagging. Men working in the woods often had to take off at top speed, and if a pant leg caught, it could mean the difference between life and death.

Figure 18. Loggers wear cutoff pants—an interesting detail, explained by the label, which might otherwise go unnoticed.

Verbs are important tools. They vividly communicate action and meaning. This example comes from the caption for a totem pole:

> The totem poles that stood in front of houses of the Northwest Pacific Coast Indians symbolized family heritage and status. Family crests, handed down through generations, depicted animals, mythical beings, and incidents from legends.

The central message is contained in the verbs: stood, symbolized, depicted.

Let verbs work for you. Avoid the tradition of beginning every other sentence with "This is" and "These are." Indeed, avoid the verb "to be" in all its forms—is, are, was were, will be—and substitute an active verb whenever possible. Three more good examples:

> The fur trade lured settlers to the waterways which connected the Great Lakes with the fur-rich hinterlands of the Midwest.

> *Gorgosaurus*, a powerful flesh eater, towers over *Lambeosaurus*, a vegetarian, exhibited in its actual death pose.

> Using their beaks to plaster mud, the mated pair of hornbills seals the female inside the nest box, leaving a hole just large enough for her beak to stick out.

Make your verbs active, and your sentences will radiate the life of the objects themselves and of the people who created them. As Zinsser says about verbs in his book *On Writing Well*, "They push the sentence forward and give it momentum. Active verbs push hard; passive verbs tug fitfully" (p. 102).

Long sentences make reading more difficult, and therefore they should be avoided. It is all right to write long sentences in the first draft, when you are putting ideas on paper, but pare them down later. Vary the length of the sentences and the length of the labels. All captions should not conform to one exact size. Leave some white space on your labels occasionally. You do not need to fill all the space just because it is there. Chapter 4 discusses sentence length in greater detail.

The three guidelines that I suggest are basically common sense. Some writers intuitively know to use visual, active language and short sentences, but many labels lack them. A recent traveling exhibition contained a sentence in the introductory paragraph which was ninety-six words long! When will we learn?

The Second Draft

Let the first draft sit overnight or several days before you review it. This step assumes that you have allowed ample time for the label-writing process and that the exhibit is not scheduled to go up this afternoon. Remember: the more time you give to preparing labels, the more time your visitors will spend with them.

Read over the first draft with an "innocent eye," pretending that you have never seen it before. How does it sound? Read it out loud. Is it smooth? Does it make sense? Does it make you want to look at the exhibit it talks about? Make changes whenever there is any doubt about clarity.

Strive for a good balance between confidence and self-criticism at this point. Too much confidence can lead to embarrassing moments later when your editor asks, "What are you talking about?" On the other hand, if you are overly critical, you may bog down in agony over every word. Rely on your first impulses, but do not regard your words as final yet. Stay flexible, but hold onto your opinions. If you grow stale on the copy, it helps to show it to someone else for a fresh point of view.

Styles to Avoid

Often people liken writing labels to writing advertising copy. Certainly there are some similarities; both strive to catch attention and to "sell" a message. There is, however, a poor advertising style, which labels should not try to imitate, and other styles which are simply not appropriate. Avoid, for example, two of the most common devices: (1) the use of incomplete sentences, and (2) sentences that begin with "and" and "or." The following example comes from an ad for a wristwatch.

Its character is unmistakable, whether it's worked in 18 karat yellow gold. Or steel. Or even a striking combination of gold and steel.

The words sound choppy and unnatural. This style is too casual for most labels. Labels represent the written, not the spoken, word (unless the spoken word is being directly quoted).

Knowing When to Stop

The number of drafts will vary with the amount of copy, complexity of concepts, and time available. It is not unusual for a 100-word label to go through seven drafts even before it is tried with the visitors. By allowing adequate time for drafts and editing, you will have better copy when the moment arrives for production.

The time to stop writing is when you are convinced that you have met your stated objectives. Again, the value of having objectives for each label cannot be overstressed. They provide the focus and the restraint necessary for writing good, short labels. Without objectives, you will not be certain to know when to stop, and the temptation to "tell 'em everything" will get out of control.

Editing

Some people do not like to be edited. They regard their words as precious and feel that editors are insensitive barbarians. Some people do not realize that they write poorly.

Label writers should look upon editors as their friends, people who have the same interest at heart: making sure that the writer communicates the message. Authors can edit and proofread their own copy only to a point, after which editing can be not only difficult but dangerous. Authors know what they wanted to say and will see it even if it is not on the page. An editor does not have that prejudice and can easily spot troublesome areas.

Editing means making changes to improve clarity, meaning, and style. Some changes are only minor, whereas others may be quite substantial. Different activities lead to editorial changes:

1. proofreading—to make sure the copy is free of errors in matters such as spelling, punctuation, and word order;
2. content editing—to make sure the meanings are distinct and the copy is the correct length. If long copy has to fit a short space, condensing is necessary;
3. testing—to make sure that the copy's meaning is clear to the audience for which it is intended.

Spelling errors have an insidious way of persisting all the way to final production and installation, where visitors will immediately spot them. Proofreading for spelling and grammar should be done by someone skilled in these areas. Many good writers are not good spellers—the talents are not necessarily linked. When you are proofreading it is a good idea to use two people—one can read aloud from the original copy while the other person silently checks the retyped or typeset version. Missing words, lines, or even paragraphs will be discovered more quickly this way. If you are alone, you can read to yourself using a tape recorder.

Editing can involve major reconstruction, deletions, or suggestions that aim to clarify meaning. Museum labels often make it necessary to shorten copy to fit a given space, and good editing can help by refining writing to its essentials, eliminating extraneous material. The final version may contain fewer facts than the original, and many authors will squirm at deletions, but everyone will appreciate the results—clean, crisp copy. Note in the following captions for a zoo raccoon how jumbled and encyclopedic the first sample is, compared with the second:

Writing Copy

Seventy-nine words:
Known for their intelligence and ability to manipulate objects with their front paws, raccoons typically live alone. Active at night, they eat many different types of vegetable and animal foods but have a special fondness for crayfish taken from shallow water along rivers and streams. Their scientific name "lotor" refers to the habit in caged raccoons of sometimes putting their food in water. Apparently they do this not to wash it but to be able to "rediscover" it there.

Thirty-three words:
Raccoon's favorite food is crayfish. Caged raccoons sometimes put their food in water before eating it—not to wash it but apparently to "rediscover" it there, as if it were a living crayfish.

Another form of editing can be done partly by visitors. If possible, labels should be tried out with visitors before final production, especially if the final form is expensive. If errors are discovered before copy is fixed in type, there is time for changes. Then, too, if your words—which seemed so good on paper at your desk—fail to communicate, you will want to revise once again. The process of trying out labels will make you more aware of your visitors as readers. Editors can provide one service for writers, but it is the average visitor's opinion that ultimately measures effectiveness. Chapter 4 describes techniques for trying out labels. The process takes time but is worth it. If you cannot test all of the labels, at least test some of the more important ones.

Marking Copy for Production

Copy must be specially marked before it is set in type. A set of symbols called proofreaders' marks is used to tell the typesetter how to set the copy (pamphlets by Gore and Alderson, listed in the bibliography, provide a complete discussion). Some marks indicate the style of type to be used, the amounts of space called for, and the length of dashes, for example. Proofreaders' marks also offer a neat and unambiguous means of correcting errors in proof, which usually has less room for written changes than the typed page does. Some knowledge of typesetting and printing is useful in understanding how to prepare copy for production, and we will consider these matters next.

3

Composition
and Printing

When label copy is in final form, production begins. In many cases this last stage involves merely typing the copy on a card. In other cases, production may involve several mechanical and artistic steps before the label is completed. Whatever the method, certain fundamentals should be observed.

All labels should be produced according to the principles of good typography. The term "typography" denotes the style, arrangement, and appearance of typeset copy; also, the effective and pleasing use of type is often described as "good typography" (see figure 19). Label writers must be typographers—in the sense that they must know some basic steps and rules of thumb. A clear and concise message can be rendered unreadable by any number of small but significant errors that may be substantive or typographic. The writer must check and correct the copy at each stage, even though other professionals, such as artists and designers, may be involved in the production process.

There are many ways of producing labels by hand: typewriters, stencils, block printing, silk screen, calligraphy, and dry-transfer letters are some of the methods that have been used, and a number will be discussed in chapter 5. Professional typesetting yields predictably pleasing and professional results, however, and label writers should know how to find and to use the available services. An appreciation of good typography calls for some knowledge of how type is set, beginning with the distinction between typesetting, or composition (the assembling of letters to be reproduced), and printing (a word that properly refers to the reproduction of copies). Some historical knowledge of printing and composition is also desirable, since many common terms have a traditional significance that may not be apparent from modern usage.

A Brief History of Printing Type

Printing type was first developed by the Chinese but did not come into widespread use, partly for cultural reasons and partly because of the complexity of the Chinese alphabet. In East and West the printed book as we know it was preceded by development of the arts of calligraphy,

Figure 19. Typography—the style, arrangement, or appearance of typeset matter—is a useful art. It is not a fine art, but there is such a thing as fine typography, and museum labels should exemplify it. Here we see typography as the subject of fine art. One interpretation of the painting is its celebration of the form and balance of letters, numerals, and punctuation.

illumination, and block printing. These were slow methods indeed, although block printing did permit reproduction in quantity.

The invention of movable type in the West is usually attributed to Johann Gutenberg. In about 1450 he used a machine resembling a wine press to print directly from a raised, inked surface of metal type. The letters could be cleaned, resorted, and reused. Within fifty years the invention had spread to every major country.

Although printing was greatly speeded by the end of the sixteenth century, it was still slow, depending on the rapidity with which a human typesetter could form a line of copy by hand. The nineteenth century, however, saw the invention of the revolutionary Linotype (1886; its competitor, the Intertype, followed in 1911). This was a keyboard-operated machine that could cast a line of type at a time from molten metal. The Monotype, created in 1887–88, consisted of two machines, one of which generated a perforated paper tape and the other of which read the tape and cast the type. Whereas the Linotype produced a solid line, or slug, of type, the Monotype cast individual characters. (The Ludlow Typograph, developed in 1906, offered handset linecast copy in larger, "display," sizes.)

The basic printing processes are four. In letterpress, a raised surface of type prints directly onto paper, and before the development of solid printing plates proofs had to be checked not only for accuracy but also to determine the evenness of the printing surface. A second, indirect method, offset lithography, was perfected in the 1920s and now involves the transfer (or offset) of the printed image from a photomechanically prepared printing plate to a rubber blanket before it encounters paper. This means of printing from a flat surface reduces wear and tear on plates and permits copies to be made more rapidly. Another form of printing, the rotogravure familiar from Sunday supplements, uses an incised plate. In this case the ink lies in recesses below the plate's surface and is transferred to paper by suction. The fourth major printing process, silk screen, will be discussed separately in chapter 5.

The increasing mechanization of typesetting has brought a proliferation of typefaces since the earliest days of movable type. Names such as Garamond, Baskerville, Caslon, and Bodoni recall the men whose designs—originating in the 1600s and 1700s— are still popular today. Before 1878 typefaces were not standardized; different foundries produced type of different sizes, and the fonts sold by one firm were likely to be incompatible with those made somewhere else. The advance of technology in the late nineteenth century necessitated a more uniform approach. About 1878 printers adopted standard units—points and picas—for measuring the size of type, lines, spaces, and borders. Additional changes took place as the industry became more specialized and its equipment more sophisticated.

The twentieth century is witnessing another revolution in typesetting, the invention of new methods (and new typefaces) for "cold type" composition, so called because no hot metal is used. Photocomposition, introduced in 1949, has been especially successful. One method makes words by exposing film to light passed through a film template of letter forms. The film is processed inside the machine and reproduction-quality copy is produced on film or on photographic paper (there are no intermediate proof stages). Other, newer methods employ digital computers and cathode ray tubes that scan characters onto film at the rate of 600 lines per minute. Because the cost of typesetting is always directly related to the amount of manual work involved, attention is also being given to electronic devices that read typewritten copy, altogether eliminating the need for a keyboard.

Some museums may prefer to use hand lettering (see figure 20) for their labels, which adds a personal touch. The revolution in the typesetting industry, however, means that high-quality composition is available at relatively low cost. The advent of new equipment and technology also means that museums should think twice before buying or accepting as a gift obsolete machines whose routine maintenance may require skilled operators and parts that

Figure 20. Neatly hand-lettered labels can be legible, too.

are difficult or expensive to obtain. Finally, purchasing phototypesetting may prove less costly than time- and labor-intensive methods of producing labels, especially if the cost-benefit ratio takes into account the greater legibility and professional quality that technology has made possible. Too often the costs of producing labels are not weighed against the "costs" of *not* spending money on them.

The Language and Fundamentals of Typography

When labels contain only words (no artwork), good design means good typography. Because drawings, photographs, or other art is added to relatively few museum labels, we will concentrate on labels which use words alone. (Interesting graphic use of art, however, appears in many of the illustrations for this book.)

To produce labels of high professional quality, the writer must understand the language of typography. Although the terminology may seem unfamiliar at first, a brief acquaintance will lead to greater awareness and enjoyment of type.

Typeface

"Typeface" refers to the design, form, or shape of the letters within an alphabet. When you choose typefaces for museum labels, foremost considerations should be given to legibility and availability. A few of the more common and widely available styles used in books, magazines, and newspapers include:

Bodoni	Baskerville
Caledonia	Bookman
Clarendon	Caslon
Futura	Century Schoolbook
Helvetica	Garamond
Palatino	Optima
Times Roman	Souvenir
	Univers

The method of typesetting often determines the typefaces that are available, and fashions change with time. Some typefaces enjoy periodic revival, while others may practically disappear. Most of the styles listed above are considered proven favorites: they have withstood the test of time.

Because typefaces evolved rapidly and unsystematically when printing was first invented, there was no clear system for classifying them. Rough groupings, however, are suggested by the letters' posture, thickness (or weight), and amount of decoration. Typefaces are usually first described as serif or sans serif (see figure 21). The word "serif" refers to small lines at the tips of letters that were originally made by calligraphers' brushes. Serif letters

Garamond Bold 562 – 24,36,48,60,72
ABCDEFGHIJKLMNOPQRSTUVWXYZ
abcdefghijklmnopqrstuvwxyz
1234567890(.,:;-""''?!%/ˋˊˆ˜$¢£&)
ÆÇØæœçøß

Futura Mite Medium 245 – 24,36,48 W
ABCDEFGHIJKLMNOPQRSTUVWXYZ
abcdefghijklmnopqrstuvwxyz
1234567890(.,:;-"?!$¢&)

Figure 21. Examples of fonts for Garamond (serif) and Futura (sans serif).

ABCDEFGHIJKLMNOP
abcdefghijklmnopqrstuvwx

usually show lines, or strokes, of varying thickness. Strokes that rise above the line are called ascenders; those that go below are descenders (see figure 22). Sans serif typefaces ("without the serifs") are usually of more uniform thickness than serif faces.

ABCDEFGHIJKLM
abcdefghijklmnopq

Each typeface has its own variety of forms (postures and weights) available within different "fonts" (typical fonts include regular, italic, bold, and other styles). A font usually contains 60 to 100 or more characters, with uppercase and lowercase letters, numerals, punctuation, and certain symbols. (It is sometimes necessary to order separately special characters that are not provided in a font.) Figure 23 shows the different type sizes and fonts available within the same typeface.

The slow brown fox
crawled over the awake cat.

a very young ram ran away.

Figure 22. A sentence with no descenders and a line with no ascenders.

Mixing fonts of the same typeface can add emphasis and variety to museum labels, but too much mixing should be avoided. If you mix types, mix faces that are very different. For instance, Times Roman text copy with Helvetica Bold heads would be better than Times Roman text with Century Schoolbook heads. Likewise, mixing Helvetica with another sans serif type would be poor typography. Mixing types that are too close in appearance looks like a near miss—they almost match, but do not.

If in doubt about which typeface to select, use Helvetica or Times Roman. Helvetica is especially good if you want a clinical, modern, sans-serif look. Times Roman, Century Schoolbook, or Palatino are more bookish and sometimes

The Fur Trade

"I was required to carry a pack on my back of fifty pounds weight.... These packs contained goods to exchange for furs and peltries."
Gordon Hubbard

Chicago's earliest business, the fur trade, had lured Europeans, French-Canadians, and Americans to the waterways which connected the Great Lakes with the fur-rich hinterlands of the Midwest. Using a wide variety of goods produced for exchange with Indian trappers, the traders gathered peltries that were destined for the eastern states and European markets.

To begin with, private traders like Jean Baptiste Point du Sable and John Kinzie made handsome profits at Chicago. After the War of 1812, John Jacob Astor's American Fur Company took control of the Northwest trade. By the late 1820s diminishing wildlife spelled the end of this once-flourishing enterprise.

After Raoul Varin's conception of Jean Baptiste Point du Sable. Chicago's first permanent settler. There appear to be no authentic likenesses of du Sable, a French-speaking black man who arrived in 1779 and established a prospering trading post on the north bank of the Chicago River.
Reproduction from an engraving by Charles C. Dawson after an aquatint by Raoul Varin, 1930.

Figure 23. Several different type sizes as well as the use of bold and italics—within the same typeface—gives an interesting label.

more formal. All are readable and safe. When you become more expert, experiment with different types, but be aware that the best museum designers often use only one type. When Willis Shell, a noted typographer was asked "What is your current favorite type?", he replied "Well, I've been using Caslon for the last 40 years, but when I exhaust its possibilities, I'm thinking of switching to Baskerville."

Type Size

Every letter sits on an invisible baseline, and type sizes are measured in relation to that baseline:

- The distance from the baseline to the top of the highest point in the alphabet plus the distance from the baseline to the lowest point in the alphabet tells you the overall vertical measurement, or point size (figure 24).
- The height of a typical capital letter is called the H-height.
- The height of a typical lowercase letter, excluding ascenders or descenders, is called the x-height.

The traditional units of type measure are points and picas. A point is equal to 0.0138 inches, and there are approximately seventy-two points to an inch. A pica is a shorthand measurement for twelve points. One pica equals approximately one-sixth of an inch.

Type sizes are usually given in points. The smallest type

Figure 24. H-height and x-height measured in points, picas, inches, and millimeters. Type size indicates overall size, including ascenders and descenders. H-height and x-height measure the height of a capital and a lowercase letter from the baseline up.

47

size in common use is six point. "This is 6-point type." Line length is traditionally expressed in picas. Most books, magazines, and newspapers use eight- to twelve-point type for text. Books printed for the visually impaired ("large print" books) use fourteen- or eighteen-point type. Eighteen- to seventy-two-point type is used for headlines and for advertising copy.

This is 30-pt. type.

As figure 24 shows, the dimensions of type may be expressed in three quite distinct ways: in terms of (1) H-height, (2) x-height, or (3) type size. Different typefaces and different fonts show differences in the proportions of characters. Although the H-heights of two typefaces of the same point size may be nearly identical, for example, the x-heights may be different.

This type is 18-point Garamond.

This type is 18-point Century.

Although smaller sizes of type are usually specified in points, larger display type may be specified in inches (particularly in the case of ready-made press-apply letters, to be discussed shortly). When you buy typesetting services you will need to know whether the size you have in mind refers to the type size or to the H-height. In addition, it is important to remember that the more commonly used typefaces have been redesigned for use with different methods of composition. Variations in size having to do with new typesetting technologies are a potential source of confusion.

To help you assess and compare typefaces, some typesetters and suppliers of prepared lettering offer type specimen books, and conversion charts indicate how they have translated traditional sizes. The chart supplied by Transfertech, a manufacturer of dry-transfer lettering, is shown below.

	Capital height	
Point size	Millimeters	Inches
72	19.050	3/4
60	15.875	5/8
48	12.700	1/2
36	9.525	3/8
24	6.350	1/4
18	4.763	3/16
14	3.705	7/48
12	3.175	1/8

Type is specified in points and picas in the United States, England, and Canada. The European system differs from that used in the United States, and there may be some movement toward general conversion to a metric system.

Time, knowledge, and experience of the trial-and-error sort are needed to develop typographic skills. If this subject is new to you and you feel confused, do not despair. It takes time to feel comfortable with typography. Read, ask questions, and experiment. You can learn from talking with designers and typesetters, and the bibliography at the end of this book suggests general sources that will help you. The more informed you are, the better the results you will obtain.

Type that is smaller than twelve points is collectively called "text," or book, type. Type larger than twelve points is called display type because it is most often associated with headlines and advertising (see figure 25). The most frequently used (and available) sizes of display type are fourteen, eighteen, twenty, twenty-four, thirty, thirty-six, forty-eight, sixty, and seventy-two points.

Museums are "cross-breed" users of type in that they construct (or design) labels like text but make them in display sizes. Museum labels should not confuse their uses of display type with the techniques of advertising copy. Advertisements are aimed at attracting attention, and doing so often means breaking the rules of good typography.

Figure 25. The display type on this title panel suggests the nature of each exhibit.

Unusual alignment, letters that are extra bold, characters that crowd or overlap each other, and strange or ornate typefaces may catch the eye more effectively than normal type. Attractiveness should be balanced by legibility, however: design must always serve content.

Museum labels are concerned with holding attention, not with attracting it (except perhaps in title labels). The objects on display provide the drawing power, and viewers who choose to read should find labels suitably placed and conforming to the principles of legible lettering (see chapter 4). The label design should not distract attention from the message. In general, the longer the text, the more important legibility becomes.

When choosing a typeface, make sure it is available in the sizes you need and in both capital and lowercase letters. Often only capital letters are available in the larger sizes—the assumption being that display sizes are used only for headlines, titles, and the like. Copy longer than about fifteen to twenty words is difficult to read if it is set completely in capital letters, or "full caps." See figure 26.

If larger sizes are not available in both capital and lowercase, it is possible to use smaller type sizes and then enlarge them photographically to the size needed. Starting with the size you have (100 percent), the formula is: divide the size you want by the size you have and multiply by 100;

the result is the percentage of enlargement. For example, if you have ⅛ inch and you want ¼ inch,

$$(¼ \div ⅛) \times 100 = \textbf{200 percent enlargement}$$

To reduce sizes, reverse the formula. For example, if you have ½ inch and you want ¼ inch,

$$(¼ \div ½) \times 100 = \textbf{50 percent reduction}$$

Letters enlarged more than 200 percent tend to become coarse in appearance; letters reduced more than 50 percent may become too fine and may start to fill.

Justification

The lengths of typewritten lines tend to be different because there are rarely the same number of letters and spaces in each line. When all the lines are made the same length by changing the spacing, the copy is termed justified right and left.

Even margins are said to be flush, and justified copy is "flush left and flush right." Copy can be set with an even margin on the left, leaving an uneven margin on the right ("ragged right"); see figure 27. Copy can also be set ragged left or with each line centered (both margins would then appear ragged).

Body copy is usually fully justified or set ragged right,

DROMEDARY CAMEL
Camelus dromedarius
NORTH AFRICA AND ARABIA

THE DROMEDARY CAMEL ALONG WITH ITS COUSIN, THE BACTRIAN OR TWO-HUMPED CAMEL, IS AMONG THE LARGEST OF THE EVEN-TOED HOOFED MAMMALS. ASIDE FROM SERVING AS BEASTS OF BURDEN IN THEIR HOMELANDS, THE CAMELS ALSO ARE UTILIZED AS SOURCES OF MEAT, MILK, CLOTHING, AND SHELTER (USING THE HIDE) IN ADDITION, THE DUNG IS USED AS HEATING FUEL DURING THE WINTER. QUITE CONTRARY TO POPULAR THOUGHT, THE CAMEL'S HUMP IS NOT A RESERVOIR FOR WATER, RATHER IT IS USED FOR THE STORAGE OF FAT. THE TRUE MEANS BY WHICH THE CAMEL CAN GO FOR DAYS WITHOUT A DRINK IN ITS SWELTERING DESERT ENVIRONMENT INVOLVES A COMPLEX SERIES OF BODILY PROCESSES. UNLIKE ITS TWO-HUMPED RELATIVE WHICH IS REPRESENTED BY BOTH DOMESTIC AND WILD POPULATIONS, THE DROMEDARY CAMEL IS EXTINCT IN THE WILD. THE DOMESTIC FORM HAS BEEN SO FREQUENTLY MOVED ABOUT FOR THE BENEFIT OF MAN THAT ITS ORIGINAL RANGE CAN NEVER BE PERFECTLY KNOWN. IT IS THOUGHT THAT ITS DOMESTICATION TOOK PLACE IN ARABIA AS EARLY AS 4,000 B.C.

Figure 26. This label—with centered type, all capitals, and no paragraphs—is not very easy to read.

The length of typewritten lines tend to be different because there are rarely the same number of letters and spaces in each line. When all the lines are made the same length by changing the spacing, the copy is termed justified right and left. Even margins are said to be flush, and justified copy is "flush left and right." Copy can be set with an even margin on the left, leaving uneven margin on the right ("ragged right"). Copy can also be set ragged left or with each line centered (both margins would then appear ragged).

The length of typewritten lines tend to be different because there are rarely the same number of letters and spaces in each line. When all the lines are made the same length by changing the spacing, the copy is termed justified right and left. Even margins are said to be flush, and justified copy is "flush left and right." Copy can be set with an even margin on the left, leaving uneven margin on the right ("ragged right"). Copy can also be set ragged left or with each line centered (both margins would then appear ragged).

The length of typewritten lines tend to be different because there are rarely the same number of letters and spaces in each line. When all the lines are made the same length by changing the spacing, the copy is termed justified right and left. Even margins are said to be flush, and justified copy is "flush left and right." Copy can be set with an even margin on the left, leaving uneven margin on the right ("ragged right"). Copy can also be set ragged left or with each line centered (both margins would then appear ragged).

The length of typewritten lines tend to be different because there are rarely the same number of letters and spaces in each line. When all the lines are made the same length by changing the spacing, the copy is termed justified right and left. Even margins are said to be flush, and justified copy is "flush left and right." Copy can be set with an even margin on the left, leaving uneven margin on the right ("ragged right"). Copy can also be set ragged left or with each line centered (both margins would then appear ragged).

Figure 27. Samples of different margins: justified; ragged right; ragged left; and centered.

and such lines are the easiest to read. Our eyes are accustomed to returning to the same point at the left when we begin reading the next line. Ragged right copy is sometimes preferable to justified for museum labels, because it allows for even word spacing. A block of copy that is not completely squared has a more informal appearance.

For legibility's sake, museum labels should conform to familiar practices. Label readers are already at a disadvantage because of unusual reading distances and type sizes, and they do not need the added aggravation of odd typography. Use ragged left only for short amounts of copy (fewer than fifty words), and save centered copy for only the very briefest announcements and headings.

End-of-line hyphenation is familiar to all readers of books, magazines, and newspapers, where there is an emphasis on filling the available space with as many words as possible. Justification is easier if words can be divided at the ends of lines.

In museum labels, where filling all the available space may not be necessary or desirable, ragged right reduces the need to break words. Copy without end-of-line hyphens, especially in display type sizes, is easier to read, because the reader does not have to remember the first part of the hyphenated word during the longer-than-normal time it takes the eye to travel back to the beginning of a line of large type. Skilled typesetters adjust space between words so as to minimize hyphens at the ends of lines.

If you must use very short lines, set them ragged right. Bad breaks and many hyphens occur in justified lines that are too short. You can set normal or long text lines either justified or ragged right, depending on your taste, but do not set text blocks ragged left.

Letters, Words, and Space

Although letters have varying widths, most typewriters give the same amount of space on the page to each letter, resulting in different amounts of space between letters. For example, in the typed words

writing with type

there is very little space between the *w* and the *r* but lots of space between the *i* and the *t*. One of the main principles of good typography is the use of relative spacing for letters of greater or less width, so that the result is visually even letter spacing. Typesetting gives relative, or proportional, spacing to letters, as do some forms of mechanical lettering. Proportional spacing fits more characters onto a line.

number of words per line
number of words per line

Normal word spacing, whether added by eye or by machine, is about equal to the space of one letter *e* in the typeface being used. One *e* is plenty; a little less will do. Untrained typesetters (especially when working by hand) often put too much space between words, giving copy an undesirably airy and loose look. Word space, ideally, should be about the same between each word in a line. Word spacing that is exactly uniform from one line of copy to the next is generally possible only when copy is not justified on both sides.

Hand lettering methods, for example, those involving dry-transfer or adhesive-backed letters, require the user to insert space manually. The overall visual effect is most pleasing if characters are spaced proportionally, as they are when typesetting machines do the work. As a general rule, letters should not be touching, but the fit should be close. Manufacturers of dry-transfer letters usually provide guides to help the inexperienced user achieve professional results. Too much space between characters gives a clumsy, amateurish appearance, while too little space makes reading difficult.

It is occasionally desirable to add space between letters—perhaps for a special effect at the beginning of copy or to give greater prominence to a headline set in very large type. The term "letter spacing" often refers to the *addition* of such space rather than simply to the distance between characters. Some purchasers of typesetting—publishers of books and of many magazines, for example—do not permit letter spacing in text copy, although it may be used to accent subheads, titles, and the like. A typesetter may ask you whether letter spacing is permissible to facilitate justification of a line (the alternative would be to justify solely by adjusting amounts of word space). In general, you will want to avoid such letter spacing in the text of your labels, since it will mean that more space appears between letters in some words than in others. You may wish to use letter spacing throughout a headline or title, however, and if you do, the typesetter will need to know how much space to add; word space, too, will have to be increased so that words do not appear to run together. A good rule is to never letter space lower-case letters but to reserve letter spacing for lines set in all capital letters. Though some phototypesetting equipment is programmed to letter space loose lines, try to discourage it. It is better to have more space between the words.

Leading

Line spacing, or leading (pronounced "ledding"), means the amount of space between the lines of copy. Strips of lead alloy were traditionally used to separate the lines of metal type, and to "add more lead" meant putting more or thicker spacers between the lines of type. The strips were measured in point sizes, just like the letters, and the typographer's instructions might read "14 pt. with 2 pts. lead," giving a total of sixteen points from baseline to baseline ("b/b"). Although there are no rules for leading, there are recommendations based on common usage and on legibility studies (see Herbert Spencer, *The Visible Word*). In the end, depending on typeface, type size, and the kind of sign (role and content), the desirable amount of line spacing—along with other elements of the overall layout and design—may vary, depending on the exhibit situation. The term "carding" refers to the addition of space between lines to make two or more columns with different numbers of lines of equal length.

Lines without any leading are said to be "set solid," that is, the point size and the distance from baseline to baseline are the same.

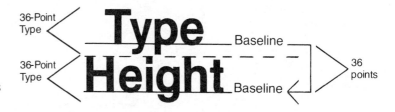

Book texts are often set in ten- or twelve-point type with one or two points of leading. In display types, as the size of the type increases, the line spacing also increases, but rarely should it exceed one and-one half times the size of the type.

As a rule of thumb, start with two points of leading for every six points of type size. If space looks too tight, increase it slightly, but avoid the mistake often made on museum labels—great gulfs are left between the lines. The reader's eyes tend to wander in the space, and the white area is out of proportion to the letters and words; see figures 28 and 29.

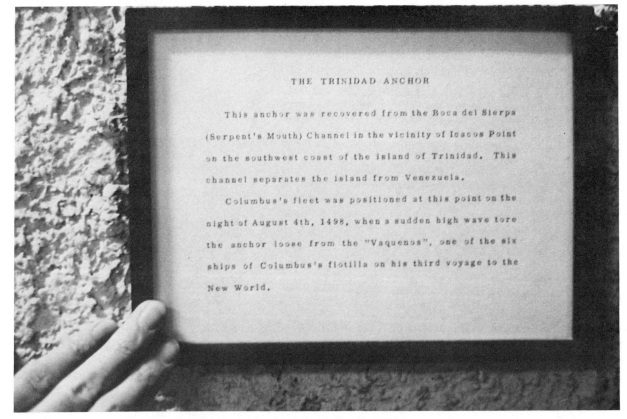

Figure 28. The space between the lines is out of proportion to the size of type.

This is a sample of eighteen-point type set with twelve points

of leading, which is too much for normal text, because

it leaves a lot of white space between the lines.

Figure 29. Lines of type with too much leading look like lines more than like groups of words.

Another rule of thumb is that long lines require more space between them than short lines. Very short lines may be set solid, but very long lines need leading between the lines. Use the two points of space for each six points of type rule for medium or long lines.

The Number of Characters per Line

The width of the label should help determine the size of the type, and the number of characters per line should not exceed sixty-five characters (spaces and punctuation count as characters, along with each letter). Words average four to six characters each, and the number of words per line will range from eight to fifteen. Very short lines— fewer than four or five words—make reading choppy. This statement is especially true in large type sizes. Try to keep the line length between forty and sixty-five characters.

Lines much longer than this are hard to read.

The larger the type size, the wider the sign needs to be.

Avoid mistakes such as planning eighteen-point type on a fifteen-inch-wide sign. Allow for margins, and leave somewhat more space at the bottom than at the top for the most balanced appearance.

Point size	Approximate line length for fifty characters (inches)
14	4½
18	• 5½
24	6½
30	8
36	10
48	13

Fitting Type

In addition to determining distance from the reader and the overall importance of the message, you must decide how big the label is to be and how many words should be used. Consider size and copy length early in the planning process. It may be preferable to start with the general design of the exhibit and to determine the optimal label sizes first. Labels should not overpower the objects displayed. Therefore size is a primary consideration. The size of the type will determine the amount of type that can fit a given space. Table 3 shows type sizes and the space needed for approximately 100 words, with line lengths of about fifty-five characters, set with normal line spaces.

Table 3. Recommended Type Sizes and Approximate Space Needed for a 100-Word Label (Including a Title) with 55 Character Lines and Normal Line Spacing

Label	Type size (points)	Space (inches)
Caption	18	7 × 4½
Caption or group	24	10 × 6
Group or introductory	36	14 × 9
Introductory	48	20 × 12

For information on more precise copyfitting—a skill in its own right—see books dealing with editing and printing that are listed in the bibliography.

Examples of ways to make type fit into interesting designs appear in some of the figures in the first two chapters of this book.

Figure 1 shows a bold lead in followed by smaller letters. Figure 2 shows a sign with centered type—best reserved for short labels, when a more formal style is desired. Figure 4 shows solid blocks of justified type and has an orderly but rather cold look. Figure 11 shows a style worth imitating: always start in the upper left corner and work down and across. This is the natural pattern for the eyes to follow. The type will always fit, even if a lot of white space is left over. Figure 15 has a casual and warm appearance—it uses a title and several lines of type set ragged right.

Figure 23, in this chapter, shows several different fonts of the same type face used together. Figure 34, in chapter 5, shows an attractive combination of words and art. Before your labels are set in type, however, you will want to assess their readability, to plan for their legibility, and to confirm their effectiveness with visitors.

Helpful Hints

1. Try to keep your line length between forty and sixty-five characters. Lines much longer are hard to read.

2. Long lines require more space between them than short lines. Very short lines can be set solid; very long lines need leading between the lines. Use the two points of space for each six points of type rule for medium or long lines.

3. Do not letter space lowercase letters. Reserve this technique for lines set in all caps. Though some phototypesetting equipment is programmed to letter space loose lines, try to discourage it. It is better to have more space between the words.

4. If in doubt about which typeface to select, use Helvetica or Times Roman. Helvetica is especially good if you want a clinical, modern, sans-serif look. Times Roman, Century Schoolbook, or Palatino are more bookish and sometimes more formal. All are readable and safe.

5. If you must use very short lines, set them ragged right because bad breaks and many hyphens appear in short justified lines. Set normal or long text lines either justified or ragged right, depending on your taste. Do not set text blocks ragged left.

6. Ask yourself how far the reader will be from the label. The further away the reader is, the larger the type must be. For a normal three and one-half foot viewing distance, use 36-point type.

7. Large blocks of type in all caps are hard to read. Reserve all caps for headings or emphasis.

8. Phototypesetting is an easy, widely available method of setting labels. Type that is keyboarded is much cheaper than type that is set by hand. Prices vary widely for photo-typeetting, so shop around and try several suppliers.

9. If in doubt, stick to one typeface for one project or exhibit. Headings or display can be created by use of larger sizes, boldface, all caps, or italics within the same family. When you become more expert, experiment with a variety of types.

10. If you must mix types, mix faces that are very different. For instance, Times Roman text copy with Helvetica Bold heads would be better than, say, Times Roman text with Century Schoolbook heads. Likewise, mixing Helvetica with another sans serif is not considered good typography. Mixing types that are too close looks like a near miss—they almost match, but do not.

11. If you must use unusual or ornate display types, use them very sparingly—only a word or two. If in doubt, avoid them.

12. Usually, you will want labels and their backgrounds to be in neutral colors which do not compete with the exhibit. Whites, blacks, grays, browns, and other subtle tones blend well with any subject.

4

Readability, Legibility, and Effectiveness

Copy and design work together to make good labels readable, legible, and effective.

Readability

Readability formulas involve counts of words, sentence lengths, and syllables to arrive at a value which indicates the relative complexity of the text (see Flesch, *How to Test Readability*). Some formulas give a measure of difficulty; others give an index of the necessary degree of reading proficiency (expressed as school grade level).

By understanding the findings of readability tests (without necessarily conducting one), you will be able to measure objectively the ease with which the copy can be read, so that your visitors will be certain to understand you. The average adult reader reads at a sixth- to eighth-grade level. Labels written at this level will be comprehensible to the majority of your visitors, will easily be translated by adults for children, and will even be read appreciatively by the youngsters themselves.

According to readability tests, decreasing the length of sentences and the number of multisyllabic words makes the text easier to read. The implication for label writers is clear: review your copy, try to shorten long sentences, and use shorter words in place of longer ones whenever possible.

The following simple formula involves two steps:

1. Check the number of words per sentence. Count all the words; divide by the number of sentences. Your sentences should ideally average between ten and twenty words.
2. Count syllables. Add up all the syllables in each label and calculate the equivalent number of syllables for 100 words. For example:
   A. You count ninety-four syllables in a sixty-seven-word label.

   94 is to 67 as X is to 100, or

   $$\frac{94}{67} = \frac{X}{100}$$

   $$X = 140$$

B. You count 178 syllables in a 110-word label.

$$\frac{178}{110} = \frac{X}{100}$$

$$X = 162$$

The range of 130 to 150 syllables per 100 words, along with an average of 10 to 20 words per sentence, is optimal for most museum labels.

Legibility

Legibility is not the same as readability, visibility, or visual acuity. These words describe different aspects of the perception and comprehension of visual stimuli and can be ranked according to the ascending complexity of mental functions required for each process.

- Visual acuity is a person's ability to see symbols. The eye doctor tests your visual acuity by asking you to read letters or symbols of a given size at a given distance.
- Visibility refers to the ease with which a symbol is seen.
- Legibility means the ease of both recognition and comprehension. Visibility is a prerequisite for legibility, but visibility tests are most often concerned with small amounts of text, such as headlines, or with the special needs of directional systems, such as traffic and highway signs—which also use short amounts of copy.

- Readability is the ease with which a reader can comprehend. It is influenced by the reader's familiarity with the content; by the writing style; by sentence length; and by the complexity of the vocabulary.

Legibility studies are concerned with perception and comprehension and focus on people's abilities to understand meanings and to recognize letters and words while reading blocks of copy. Legibility is influenced by typeface, type size, spacing, distance, color combinations, and lighting.

The elements which make type easy to see and to read have been investigated by psychologists, traffic engineers, elementary education specialists, ophthalmologists, researchers for the special needs of the handicapped, graduate students, and others. These researchers have employed a variety of methods in their investigations, ranging from tests on the effects of distance to counts of eye movements when people read and measures of rate of blinking, visual fatigue, peripheral vision acuity, and heart rate while reading. People have been studied reading material on a shaking table; ratings have been given to aesthetic preferences for different typefaces; and reading speed and comprehension have been analyzed.

Despite all the research, many museum labels are still illegible. Museum label makers may be ignorant of legibility research findings, or they may choose to ignore the findings, perhaps from a desire to be more individualistic or "creative." The legibility of museum labels could be greatly improved if their creators made use of the research results.

Findings about the legibility of book texts have broad applicability for museum labels. In fact, some of the research may have more significance for museum labels than for other forms of print. Much early legibility research was done by D. G. Paterson and M. A. Tinker (*How to Make Type Readable*). Some of their work has been criticized for lacking general relevance because they had test subjects read short, informational statements of approximately thirty words each. Their critics said that such reading differed from reading of more usual continuous copy, as in a book or newspaper. The experimenters' samples were very similar, however, to a series of museum labels.

Most of the tests used book-size type under normal reading conditions—meaning that the subjects sat while reading, and the copy was printed in eight- to twelve-point type and was suitably illuminated and held at the proper distance. Even though these "normal" conditions are not the same as those in most museum reading situations, the amount and kind of text (short and informational) make the copy similar to that found on museum labels. (Tests using street signs, catchy advertisements, or billboards would be less applicable in museum settings.) Paterson and Tinker's

conclusions, substantiated by other researchers, have resulted in a number of recommendations, which are presented below.

Choosing Type for Legibility

Avoid using ornate letters in text. Legibility is intimately associated with people's ability to recognize letters and words, and recognition is based to a great extent on familiarity. Ornate styles tend to look unfamiliar, and in bodies of copy, they make reading difficult.

Use a simple, clear typeface. Plenty are available with plain, easy-to-recognize letters. Any of the traditional or proven typefaces can be relied on for legibility.

Use roman (upright) rather than italic letters. Italics are used occasionally for emphasis, but they are not recommended for large bodies of type (see figure 30). The very difference that sets italics apart also makes reading more difficult. Museums frequently set quotations on labels in italics to suggest handwriting. For short quotations, italics can be effective, but for passages of more than fifteen words, it is better to use roman letters with quotation marks, perhaps placing the author's name in italics.

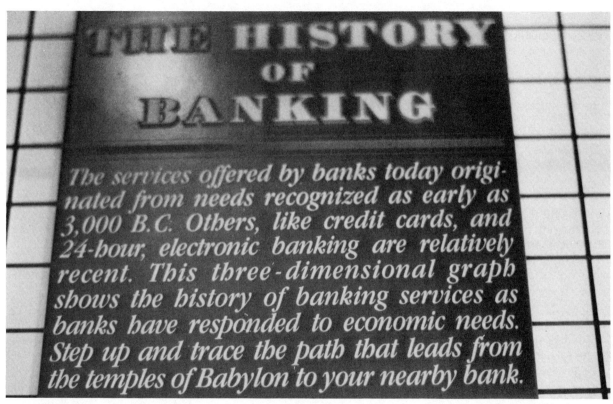

Figure 30. Italics are less legible than roman type. In this case, notice how the h almost closes at the bottom to become a b.

Use regular letters. Typefaces are easiest to read in their regular or medium (that is, medium bold) weights.

Gill Sans LIGHT   Optima

Gill Sans   **Optima** MEDIUM

Bolder faces are good for titles or headlines but are not useful in bodies of copy. For the visually impaired it is better to make type slightly larger than to make small type extra bold.

Some research has been done to determine the comparative legibility of serif versus sans serif type. Various writers say that: (1) there is a significant difference (most writers favor serif); (2) there is no significant difference; or (3) the research was not done right, and therefore the findings should be disregarded. The evidence in favor of serif says that people read words, not letters, and serif type tends to make letters in a word cohere better—that is, the serifs make the letters form more distinct words. Arguments against sans serif formerly relied on the fact that sans serif was less common, therefore less familiar and less easy to recognize and read. Most of us learned to read with serif type, yet today more children's books are being printed in sans serif type, so it is presumably more familiar than before.

The use of serif or sans serif type is largely a matter of personal preference, although there are some practical considerations as well. If you are making letters by hand, template, or dry-transfer lettering, you will probably find sans serif easier to produce. If you have type set mechanically, there are many attractive serif types to choose from.

It is best to use capitals and lowercase letters. Do not set large blocks of type in all caps; the use of full caps should be restricted to headlines or other short amounts of copy (fewer than fifteen or twenty words). Research has shown that it is more difficult to read copy that uses exclusively capital letters (see figure 26). Lines of lowercase letters are easier to recognize, even when you can only see the top half of the characters.

alphabet relates a message

Follow traditional typographical rules for spacing. Remember that letters should be close together but not touching and that words should have not more than an *e* space between them. Lines should average fifty to sixty characters, or eight to twelve words. Space between the lines should be in proportion to the type size and typeface and the line length.

The use of ragged right or justified margins is largely a matter of personal preference, and in books on typography the authors' language will give you a clue to theirs. Those in favor of justification may refer to "orderliness," or they may allude to a higher authority by saying that printing "requires" justification of lines. They may also say that a ragged right margin slows reading (not a conclusion substantiated by research). Other authors will use phrases such as "even tonal appearance" to describe ragged right and may prefer it to the "conventionally forced" uniformity of justified margins. It is interesting to note that the *Journal of Typographical Research* (now called *Visible Language*) uses both formats.

Distance, Perception, and Legibility

Normal reading distance is about twelve-fifteen inches, and normal book texts are printed in eight- to twelve-point type. At that distance, approximately four letters of that type size are projected by the lens of the eye onto the fovea of the retina—the place of clearest vision. Away from the fovea is the area of peripheral vision, which can encompass about fifteen more letters in any direction. As eyes move along a line of type, peripheral vision helps the reader anticipate what is coming into focus next. Normal reading speed averages about 250–300 words per minute, and eye movements consist of alternating sweeps and fixations along a line of type, with a return sweep at the end of one line to the beginning of the next. If a person is reading less legible or less readable material, the number of fixations increases, and reading speed decreases. The reader may also have to go back over the same line twice to correct inadequate perceptions.

If the size of type is increased and the reading distance is not correspondingly increased, the number of letters in focus on the fovea, and in the peripheral vision, will be decreased. Fewer letters in the field of vision decreases reading speed, because the eyes must make more fixations to perceive each word; that is, the reader is reading letters instead of reading words. This process can be very tiring. In addition, because the eyes and the brain are "geared" to an expected or normal reading speed/perception, slowing the eyes allows time for the brain to become distracted. The reader experiences difficulty concentrating.

There is little reason to use type larger than thirty-six points for group labels or captions, because most people prefer to stand fairly close to such labels as they examine displays. If readers can stand within two feet of the labels, smaller type sizes such as eighteen or twenty-four point may be used. To readers only two feet away, thirty-point type will seem to scream.

Full-sized examples of twenty-, thirty-six-, and forty-eight-point type in black on white and vice versa appear at the end of this chapter. Hold up these samples in your exhibit area to see how legible they appear at different distances.

For greatest legibility, follow these additional suggestions.

1. Make the size of the type proportional to the expected reading distance (see figures 31 and 32).

Type size	Maximum comfortable Reading Distance (feet)
12	1.5 feet
18	2.25 feet
24	3 feet
30	3.75 feet
36	4.5 feet
48	6 feet
60	7.5 feet
72	9 feet

2. Keep distant labels short. Labels placed at greater distances must compete with many more distractions in a person's peripheral vision.

3. Use the recommended amounts of leading between lines so that peripheral vision can include the next line down during reading of the previous line, making reading easier.

Dark type against a light background is easier to read than the reverse. From the standpoint of legibility, black type against a white or buff background is the best choice. White type is acceptable for headlines or very short amounts of copy. In reverses (white on black), sans serif type may work better than serif. White type is used in newer museum exhibits because it allows designers to use vividly colored backgrounds uninterrupted by blocks with white-background labels. White letters are often silk-

The optical quality of white type against a dark background makes it tiring to read if the label is more than 20 words long.

screened directly onto colored surfaces. Keep in mind that the most visible combinations of color, however, are not necessarily the most legible: striking appearance is different from legibility. School bus labels—in black printed against a yellow background—are both highly visible and highly legible, but few designers would choose those colors, preferring to keep labels as low-key elements in the exhibit design.

Figure 31. An exhibit combines many type sizes—depending on the kind of label and the expected reading distance.

Figure 32. A hole has been worn in the bushes as people moved closer to read the small print.

Backlit labels (with light type against a dark background) are the hardest to read of all. Their optical qualities strain the eyes, even when the proper filters or color screens are used. The letters seem to move back and forth or vibrate, a distraction even dedicated readers will find tiring. Only the shortest possible amounts of copy should be prepared for backlit displays. Keep paragraphs to twenty-five words or fewer, and use medium-weight sans serif letters.

Considering the Handicapped

People in wheelchairs have lines of sight that are considerably lower than those of the temporarily able bodied (TABs). The former will not be able to see labels which are small and high or are placed flat on a raised surface. If your museum must use such labels, consider making a second, portable set which handicapped persons may borrow while viewing the exhibits.

Many people with impaired vision can read fourteen- to eighteen-point medium-weight serif letters. Consider eighteen-point type to be the minimum size for caption and ID labels, even for visitors with normal sight, and use twenty-four- to thirty-six-point type for group and introductory labels. Enlarged periods and commas also make reading easier, as does eliminating hyphens.

Sighted persons accompanying blind visitors may be willing to read labels to them. Labels should be written to sound pleasant when read aloud. Braille labels should contain the same information as the printed labels, so that blind visitors can read for themselves without feeling cheated of information. A Chicago-based organization, Horizons for the Blind (7001 North Clark, Chicago, Illinois 60626), has helped many museums to adapt their services for blind and partially sighted visitors.

Ameslan, or American sign language, is a direct and literal form of communication. Deaf readers (especially children) may be confused by labels written in the passive voice or with abstract and technical language. Simple declarative sentences are best in copy intended for the deaf. Compare these samples of Ameslan translations with the original script of an audiovisual program at an aquarium:

Original	Ameslan
Radiating from the central rotunda are six exhibition galleries.	Around center six different rooms.
Directly behind the display tanks are 95 reserve tanks which hold extra specimens.	Behind can't see have 95 water boxes for other fish.

The things you do to make labels better for your handicapped visitors, such as providing larger type, good placement, interesting reading, and clear writing, will make labels better for *all* your patrons.

Although there are no absolute rules for maximum legibility, we have seen that many factors can contribute to making type more legible. Decisions made for achieving the best design may not be the same as decisions for best legibility, and each museum has to consider its own set of conditions and variables to arrive at suitable compromises.

Testing Effectiveness

By testing a label on a small sample of visitors you can objectively determine how effectively the label will communicate with the whole audience. Such tests, known as "formative evaluation," may suggest desirable changes when they are still easy and inexpensive to make. You should choose a sample that is a cross section of all visitors, not just thirty-two-year-old males, for example, or elderly couples, unless your labels are meant for that audience only. It is not necessary to use huge samples. For your test you will usually need only one-half to one hour and fewer than twenty-five people. If the label is not working with the first six visitors, it is not necessary to try it with ten more people before you make changes.

Random Sampling

When testing new labels before production, or when measuring reactions of visitors to a finished exhibit, you should choose visitors on the basis of a systematic sampling technique. The reason for doing so is to avoid subconsciously selecting only a certain type of visitor. All visitors during a sampling period should have equal probability of being picked.

Try to get a "random" sample—every fifth visitor, every tenth person, or even all visitors during the sampling period. Your sample will rarely be truly random, because not all visitors to the museum will visit the exhibit or the area where the label is posted. Unless you can recruit visitors at the front door of the museum, you will have to settle for a semirandom sample. When doing formative evaluation, a casual approach is acceptable. If you were doing more formal research, you would follow a stricter set of rules.

The labels that you are testing should ideally be accompanied by the objects they describe, since it is difficult to determine effectiveness otherwise. At a minimum the test labels should be placed in areas relating to the exhibit's topic or near a picture of the objects that will be displayed.

Three Testing Techniques

There are three basic techniques for trying out labels: interviews with cued readers, interviews with uncued readers, and unobtrusive observations of uncued readers.

The cued reader. Take a neatly written copy of the proposed label into the public area. Ask several visitors (randomly selected) to read it aloud (so that you can judge their familiarity with the words) and to give you an opinion.

Unfortunately, this method has a serious drawback: it puts people on the spot. Adults may be embarrassed if they cannot read a difficult word, or they may be reluctant to cooperate for some other reason. Also, they will tend to be overly complimentary; they do not want to complain or to sound critical. After all, you are the professional, and they will want to say what they think you want to hear. Sixth-grade children are good "targets" for this testing method, because they are usually more used to reading aloud, more candid, and less shy than most adults.

The uncued reader. Post the label in a logical spot, that is, near the objects to which the label refers. A piece of paper taped to a wall will attract more attention than an ordinary label, but do not worry about this "novelty effect" right now. (It would make a difference if you were measuring attraction rates, but you are concerned only with readability and comprehension right now.) Wait until someone reads the label and then walks away. Intercept the person, introduce yourself and your purpose, and ask a few questions? Did he or she read the label? (When visitors have been observed looking in the direction of a label with a sustained gaze for more than five seconds, the probability that they will answer yes to this question is about 95 percent.) Does the person remember what the label said? Was it understandable? Does the visitor have any questions? If readers can recall what was said—or can even quote from it—you have evidence of short-term learning and retention. If they do not remember, or did not take the main point, you need to make some modifications and try again.

The big difference between this method and the first one is that the uncued reader is a *spontaneous* reader; by contrast, using the first technique you may stop a visitor who under normal circumstances would not be likely to read. For which audience are you writing labels—all potential readers or all actual readers? By combining the two techniques, you can sample the responses of both kinds of visitors. Remember that no label will be successful for all visitors. You should be striving for comprehension and enjoyment by the average reader, that is, by six to eight people out of ten. Each sign will have a slightly different audience and rate of attraction, so set your standards accordingly.

Unobtrusive observations. Before testing, calculate the

number of words and the anticipated reading time. For example, a 100-word label written at a sixth-grade level should take the average reader about twenty seconds to finish.

Post the label as before, but this time do not approach readers. Just observe, and make notes on every person who reads. How long does each read (number of seconds spent staring at the label), and what does each do during and after reading? Place yourself with a stopwatch in a position where you can see the visitor's face without being conspicuous as an observer. If it becomes apparent that the person is aware of being watched, terminate that sequence and wait for another subject.

Record the reading times of about a dozen people. If most of them look at the label long enough to read it all, the copy is probably not too long. If very few people read it at all or finish it, you have problems. It may be too long or too dull. Take the label down, rewrite it, and try again.

Notice also what people do while they read. Do they stop and look and then read more? Do they point at the copy or read it out loud to a friend? If the label is meant to contain a bit of humor, do they laugh? Unobtrusive observations can reveal certain aspects of visitors' reactions that are not normally apparent in interviews. This method checks for what visitors *do*, producing results that can be compared with what visitors *say*.

The Results of Research

Larger sampling sizes, more systematic sampling techniques, and controlled variables distinguish summative evaluation and effectiveness research from formative evaluation. Research strives to uncover the reasons why one thing is more effective than another and to make generalization and prediction possible. By contrast, formative evaluation seeks to determine whether an effort is effective at all. Does it make much difference if one label has shorter sentences, more active verbs, and more visual content and is simpler to read than another? Research has shown that it does indeed.

At a zoo exhibit of fruit bats, only 5 percent of the visitors who stopped at the windows to observe the bats read the label. It was in a poor location, too far from the windows, and the writing began traditionally: "This species is . . . These fruit bats are . . ." When the label was moved to a better location, readership increased to 14 percent. A new label—similar in size, color, and placement—contained a catchy title and active verbs and was easier to read. It made readers of 56 percent of all who stopped—an increase of 42 percent.

The walrus label contained 218 words. Visitors were observed to read the label for an average of twenty-three seconds. It was estimated that twenty-three seconds was not enough time to read the entire label if the average reading speed was five words per second. A new label was prepared containing 179 words with more visual and concrete information. The design of both labels and the average number of words per sentence were the same. Readers spent an average of thirty-one seconds with the new label. These data suggested that viewers were reading 34 percent more of the new text than of the old (see table 4).

Table 4. The Holding Rate of the Walrus Labels

	Old label	New label
Words	218	179
Reading time (seconds)	23	31
Text read (%)	53	87

In a natural history museum, visitors were given a multiple-choice quiz after they had read one of two dinosaur labels and had viewed the display. Reading was spontaneous and uncued. After being observed reading, the visitors filled out a "questionnaire." One label was considered difficult, that is, it had long sentences, technical words, and abstract concepts. The other, easy label used the same number of words but contained fewer words per sentence, fewer technical terms, and more concrete information. They both contained the same facts. Visitors who had read the easy label scored significantly better on the quiz than readers of the difficult label. Visitors who had not read either label scored significantly lower than visitors who had read the difficult label.

Other studies have shown that reading any label can result in some learning, but less than that associated with other forms of museum education such as tours or guidebooks (see Screven, *The Measurement and Facilitation of Learning in the Museum Environment*). Since labels are often the sole form of education and interpretation available, however, it is imperative to make them as good as possible, and attracting visitors and sustaining their attention are thus crucially important.

Holding Power Reconsidered
It has often been said that visitors will not read a very long label. This statement is probably very true—for boring labels on unpopular exhibits. Some exhibits, however, have such a high amount of intrinsic interest that some visitors are willing to read even a very long label. The dinosaurs in the main hall of the Field Museum of Natural History are such an exhibit.

As an experiment, a 326-word, typewritten label was installed alongside the dinosaurs on a Saturday afternoon. In the text, five lines from the bottom, was inserted the statement "If you have read this far, please step to the desk marked visitor research and claim a small prize." A postcard was awarded to anyone who came to the desk. During a three-hour period, fourteen people asked for their reward. (To illustrate how literally some people read, some asked if the prize was a miniature dinosaur!) Several other visitors were observed reading, looking toward the desk, laughing, and walking away. On the basis of previous reading studies at the dinosaur exhibit, it was estimated that close to 15 percent of the readers were finishing the entire 326-word label. That score does not permit us to say that the average visitor read the copy completely, but certainly more than a few did so.

As these examples suggest, the amount of text that should be used in a label depends upon the type of exhibit. It may generally be true that one sort of label should be seventy-five words in length and another twenty-five, but such guidelines should not be treated as law. Objects that prompt more questions from viewers deserve greater explanations. Museum staff should learn which objects in their collection need longer labels and which objects—for the average visitor—need only a few words. Formative evaluation will help provide these data.

"Typeface" refers to the design, form, or shape of the letters within an alphabet. When you choose typefaces for museum labels, foremost considerations should be given to legibility and availability. The method of typesetting often determines the typefaces that are available. Typefaces are usually first described as serif or sans serif. The word "serif" refers to small lines at the tips of letters that were originally made by calligraphers' brushes. Serif letters usually show lines, or strokes, of varying thickness. Sans serif typefaces ("without the serifs") are usually of more uniform thickness than serif faces.

20/24 point Times Roman

The traditional units of type measure are points and picas. A point is equal to 0.0138 inches, and there are approximately seventy-two points to an inch. A pica is a shorthand measurement for twelve points. One pica equals approximately one-sixth of an inch. Type sizes are usually given in points. The smallest type size in common use is six point. Most books, magazines, and newspapers use eight- to twelve-point type for text. Eighteen- to seventy-two-point type is used for head-lines and for advertising copy.

20/24 Helvetica Regular

As a rule of thumb, start with two points of leading for every six points of type size. If space looks too tight, increase it slightly, but avoid the mistake often made on museum labels—great gulfs are left between the lines. The reader's eyes tend to wander in the

Type that is smaller than twelve points is collectively called "text," or book, type. Type larger than twelve points is called display type because it is most often associated with headlines and advertising. Museums are "cross-breed" users

36/39 point Helvetica Regular

There is little reason to use larger than thirty-six points group labels or captions, be most people prefer to stand close to such labels as they examine displays. If readers

48/50 point Times Roman

Backlit labels (with light ty
against a dark backgroun(
the hardest to read of all.
letters seem to move bacl
forth or vibrate, a distracti
even dedicated readers w

48/50 point Helvetica Regular

5

Production, Placement, and Mounting

Lettering methods available to the label maker vary in costs, not only in dollars, but also in the amounts of time required. Time and money should both be figured in the label budget. Unfortunately, there is no truly "easy" way. Every method requires skillful technique to achieve the best results.

Table 5 compares ten methods of making letters. It lists the equipment needed, initial investment, and approximate production time to produce 500 words—the amount of copy needed for one fairly long introductory label. Some methods require more steps than others. Procedural differences are noted in the table and are discussed in more detail below.

Regardless of which method you choose, certain principles of good typography must be followed to achieve legible labels. Do not begin lettering until you are thoroughly familiar with these principles (discussed in chapters 3 and 4). It is also important to remember that neat letters and proper spacing do not equal good labels. You must start with something interesting to say, then say it well and, finally, produce it legibly.

For any method, you will want to consider the relative advantages of at least a dozen different factors:

1. number of choices of typefaces;
2. choice of sizes;
3. availability of capital and lowercase letters;
4. quality of letter produced;
5. quality of photoreproduction;
6. control over letter spacing;
7. the sorts of materials on which the letters can be produced;
8. speed possible or time needed to produce;
9. initial cost, maintenance cost, materials cost;
10. ease with which the process can be learned;
11. amount of work space required;
12. setup and cleanup time.

This chapter discusses eight different methods in light of these factors, along with some of the special considerations for each case. Brand names are mentioned not in order to recommend or endorse particular products but simply as examples for purposes of illustration.

Table 5. Production Equipment, Costs, and Time for a 500-Word Label

Method	Equipment	Initial investment	Production time	Costs (not including labor)
1. Hand lettering or calligraphy	pen, ink, paper mat board	less than $100	2½ hours	less than $10
2. Typewriter	IBM Selectric with Orator element	$1,200	10 minutes (not including time to mat and trim)	less than $10
3. Mechanical lettering	Leroy	$270	2½ hours	less than $10
4. Proof press	Line-O-Scribe Morgan Sign Press	$4,365	4 hours (including clean up time)	less than $10
5. Engraved plastic	Engravograph	$1,800	3½ hours	$10 to $25
6. Headliner	KroyType	$900	2 hours for camera-ready copy	$10 to $25
7. Die Cut	Leteron	$1,200	5 hours	$10 to $25
8. Dry transfer	Letraset sheets, ruler, burnisher	less than $100	5 hours	$10 to $25
9. Hot metal typesetting	Linotype	may be free to a good home[a]	30–60 minutes	$25 or more
10. Phototypesetting	Compugraphic EditWriter	$25,000[b]	15 minutes for camera-ready	$25 or more[c]

[a]This machine is rapidly becoming obsolete.
[b]Rather than purchase such expensive equipment, museums usually contract out.
[c]Costs for all methods based on 1981 prices.

These methods deal mainly with producing type in sizes smaller than forty-eight points. For larger letters, see the methods described in Arminta Neal's *Exhibits for the Small Museum* or buy them ready made from a supplier (see chapter 6).

Typesetting

For clarity and precision, nothing can top the legibility of a clean, simple typeface set by a professional printer (see figure 33 and figure 34).

Compare the legibility of one line made by a large type typewriter with that of one typeset line.

others who may be in

I did not look back but went on

Figure 33. The Compugraphic EditWriter, a phototypesetting machine. Keyboarded words appear on the screen for editing before printout.

The shorter lines, thicker letters, proportional letter spacing, and reduced line spacing make typeset copy infinitely more readable.

Before the 1960s most typesetting was done by hot metal. Today phototypesetting does much of the work once done by hot metal composition. Phototypesetting is widely available in large cities and can be found in many smaller communities. Companies with this service range from huge syndicated operations to individuals working out of their basements. Few museums can afford their own typesetting equipment, so copy must usually be sent out. For larger jobs, such as all the copy for an entire display, the costs are very reasonable.

FOREST GLASS

Detail from *Twelve Netherlandish Proverbs*, Pieter Brueghel, 1559. Reproduction courtesy Museum Mayer van der Bergh, Antwerp.

During the Middle Ages typical glass drinking vessels were green in color because of impurities in the raw materials. Ribs and prunts were applied to help people hold the glasses securely because the custom of eating with fingers made one's hands greasy and slippery.

Figure 34. The finished product is attractive, legible, and readable.

Labels that will be set in type must be planned far ahead of time and have all their bugs worked out. Phototypesetting is not suited to last-minute jobs or to jobs requiring many changes. Because there are no true proof stages (see chapter 3), corrections—such as complete resetting or "cutting in" new patches by hand on the original typeset version—may be very expensive (sometimes double the original charge). The biggest mistake people make in buying typesetting is failing to put the typescript in final form before taking it to be set.

Typesetting results are only as good as the directions provided to the typesetter. Your setting copy should be clear, double-spaced typescript, and any corrections should be neatly printed (using uppercase and lowercase) between the lines. In addition, you must specify in writing on the copy:

1. typeface(s);
2. Point size(s) or, in the case of larger type, H-height or inch size;
3. where capital letters are to be used;
4. line length (usually in picas, but sometimes in inches); when ragged right or left is used, you should indicate the maximum and minimum acceptable line lengths;
5. whether to justify, leave ragged right margins, or center each line;
6. whether or not letter spacing is permitted in running text; if you plan to use letter spacing, you must specify where and how much, and you must also adjust the amount of word spacing, since larger gaps between words will then be needed;
7. whether or not hyphens at the ends of typescript lines are to be retained if the word is not divided in the typeset copy;
8. the amount of leading and any extra space between lines anywhere on the copy;
9. how much space should be used for paragraph indentions;
10. all fonts that will be needed (regular, italic, bold, bold italic, etc.);
11. any special symbols not included in the font that will be required;
12. which lines of copy must be set "line for line" (like poetry) rather than "run in" (like prose).

General instructions are termed specifications, or "specs."

Because the needs of museums differ from those of other buyers of typesetting, you should not assume that the compositor knows what is best, although good typesetters are willing to share their knowledge and may offer helpful suggestions. Still, only you can know what you want. Discuss the instructions and planned use of the final copy with the supplier. By learning a typesetter's capabilities you may be able to save yourself needless work. (For example, if you plan a caption label that will include a schematic diagram of your display, a trained compositor properly instructed by you can curve the typeset copy around the drawing, making it unnecessary for you to measure laboriously and specify where each line of type should end.) It is wise to include a hand-sketched layout of the approximate size and amount of copy for each label. By providing all the necessary information and directions, you can avoid unpleasant and costly surprises.

Typesetting is a prerequisite for production of professional-looking labels by many processes, such as silk screen, metal photo, Scotchcal, and photostats (discussed below). In addition, for very little expense a typeset label may be photocopied onto colored paper to produce dark letters on a colored background that will match the exhibit.

Other methods have been described in this book for setting labels, and these methods are useful, but photo-typesetting is an easy, widely available method of setting labels. For example, type that is keyboarded is much cheaper than type that is set by hand. Since prices for phototypesetting vary, shop around and try several suppliers.

Advantages of typesetting
- many choices of typefaces—usually more than fifteen available styles are appropriate for body copy;
- many type sizes available, in both capital and lowercase;
- most modern machines for setting cold type by computer have some form of "memory," and information can be stored and recalled;
- excellent letter quality for reproduction;
- proper alignment and proportional spacing.

Disadvantages of typesetting
- possible delay as you wait your turn at the typesetters;
- expensive for small jobs;
- produces black-and-white copy (or reverse) on paper or film; color backgrounds are not easily available.

Proof Printing

Museums can use any of several "proofing" machines with metal type (figures 35 and 36). One example is the Morgan Sign Press. Proofing presses are adequate for the small advertising jobs using display type in department stores. They can be adapted for museum use, but it is particularly important for the operator to use good word spacing. The machine produces professional-looking signs when correctly operated.

Figure 35. The Line-O-Scribe proof printer uses hand-set metal and wood type. Drawers ("cases") store different typefaces and sizes.

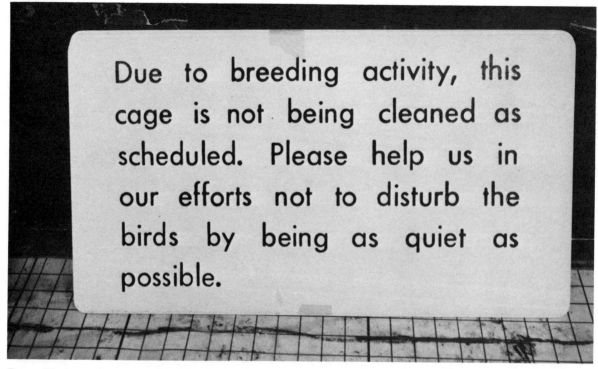

Figure 36. A proof press made this sign. The designer increased word spacing to achieve justified lines. The flatbed press makes it possible to adjust design and production easily before printing.

Proof printing involves setting type by hand. Letters are inked and are printed on paper or vinyl. This method is most useful for jobs that call for more than one copy of the same sign. The time taken to set the type, print, and clean up afterward may be impractical for one-of-a-kind signs. For instance, it takes a skilled person about three hours to produce one 100-word label and three hours and two minutes to produce two identical signs.

Advantages of the proof press
• low cost to operate and maintain;
• reasonably quick, with skilled operator.

Disadvantages of the proof press
• limited number of characters in each type size; you may have to rewrite a label if too many *e* letters needed;
• cannot print on thick, rigid surface (e.g., wood).

Engraved Plastic or Wood

"Engravograph" plastic signs are popular with some outdoor museums because these signs hold up fairly well in sun and rain. Although wood routed signs are subject to engravings other than the original text (people often add carved initials), they also last well, even in harsh weather.

The engraving machine (figure 37) drills a shallow groove into a piece of laminated plastic which is thinly covered with one color, revealing a contrasting color beneath (figure 38). The letters are drilled by following a template of the desired style and size of letter.

Advantages of engraved plastic
• durable;
• comes in a variety of colors.

Disadvantages of engraved plastic
• a mistake during production means starting over or messy corrections;
• only six type styles include both uppercase and lowercase letters.

Dry-Transfer Lettering

"Press type"—originally a brand name for dry-transfer letters—has become the generic term for this type of lettering, used in figure 39. Available in a wide choice of typefaces (in fact more styles than any museum would ever need) press type letters are purchased by the sheet. Each sheet contains multiples of all letters of the alphabet, in one font, with punctuation and numbers. (In larger size capital and lowercase letters are often supplied on separate sheets.)

Letters are rubbed off the carrier sheet onto paper or other smooth surfaces (including walls). Hold the carrier sheet absolutely steady so the letters do not break. The result can be used as is or as a master for making a photo copy.

Figure 37. Because the engraving machine has limited space, it can set large signs only three lines at a time, making composition tricky.

Figure 38. Engraved sign with centered lines—except for the last one. Most of the typefaces are available in capital letters only.

PERSONALITY

Hats reveal many things about the personality of their owners. Sometimes a hat seems to have its own personality. We offer a word descriptive of these hats. How would you describe their personalities? Dashing? Daring? Humble? Strong? Macho? Pert? Cute? Exotic? Vamp? Successful?

Figure 39. Dry-transfer letters can be applied to boards painted to match the exhibit background color. Watch out for broken letters.

Most carrier sheets have guidelines to aid proper horizontal alignment but the user must determine proper word spacing, and leading. Therein lies the problem with press type: improper spacing is common unless the letterer is experienced. Spacing for press type follows the same rules as for other forms of lettering. Although capital letters are easier to space, both capital and lowercase letters should be used for body copy, that is, for more than twenty words.

Some dry-transfer typefaces are easier to use than others. Bold, even lines are less fragile than finely sculptured letters such as Caslon. Thin letters and delicate lines break easily. Even though all capital letters are easier to line up and extra-bold letters hold together better, they leave the reader with the task of reading less legible words. The extra effort involved in using caps and lowercase medium-weight letters benefits all readers. Mistakes in press type can be lifted off gently with a piece of tape. Press-on letters applied to walls can be painted over when exhibits change.

Dry-transfer letters are fragile and become brittle with age. It is important to use only fresh letters to avoid the frustrations of crumbling, breaking letters. Purchase press type in small quantities, and use it on a first-in, first-out basis. Avoid sales on press type: the store may be trying to get rid of old stock. Choose a typeface that is popular but not trendy, so that you can buy more of it later. Different brands of the same face may not match exactly, and sizes are not absolutely consistent between brands. Try out a few different brands, pick one, and stick with it. There is a big difference between brands of dry-transfer letters in ease of transfer; some are more difficult to use than others. Again, try several brands to discover what works best for you.

Advantages of dry-transfer letters
• inexpensive initial investment;
• more than fifteen different typefaces appropriate for body copy, with many more choices of decorative styles for headlines;
• legible letters of good quality that reproduce well photographically;
• does not require tools other than a ruler or pica stick and burnisher (the cap of a ballpoint pen will do);
• mistakes are easily correctable.

Disadvantages of dry-transfer letters
• slow application, especially if you are inexperienced;
• unprofessional in appearance if proper spacing is not achieved;
• you may run out of some letters before others and may have to buy a whole new sheet to get the ones you need;
• fragility.

Die-cut letters

Made of plastic or vinyl, adhesive-backed die-cut letters are peeled from their carrier sheet and are set in place by hand. They are used mostly in headlines, or when larger letters are called for, and range in size from one-half to six inches. They can be purchased in packages containing several identical letters or on the sheet containing entire alphabets. Some companies offer preset words to order. The choices of typefaces are far fewer in die-cut letters than in press type, and most die-cut letters are available only in sizes larger than forty-eight points. Die-cut letters are durable, even outdoors, but when placed on surfaces within reach of the public, tampering fingers can peel them off.

The table-top Leteron machine (figure 40) can be used for producing die-cut letters as needed. Rolls of adhesive-backed tape, available in several colors, are loaded into the machine, and individual letters are punched into the tape, then peeled and placed on a smooth surface. Optically correct spacing is not automatic, however, and the user must peel and stick with great attention to spacing (figure 41).

Figure 40. Table-top die-cut lettering machine.

Advantages of die-cut letters
- good-looking letters;
- durability;
- colors are available;
- you can do it yourself, inexpensively.

Disadvantages of die-cut letters
- large type, not good for long text body copy;
- can be peeled off;
- few type styles.

Figure 41. To achieve optically correct letter spacing with most die-cut letters, the artist must paste down the individual letters by hand.

Figure 42. The Varityper Headliner uses photo and chemical processing. The KroyType (not shown) is a strike-on system.

The Headliner Machines

As the name implies, the headliner (figure 42) and similar machines are used primarily by graphic designers in advertising for producing short texts in display sizes. Though headliner machines are becoming obsolete, replaced by faster machines, they are relatively small, inexpensive, and easy to operate and can quickly produce letters of good quality that are suitable for photo reproduction. Letter spacing is adjustable (figure 43).

Headliner typefaces, fonts, and sizes are controlled by discs. Separate discs are needed for each font and size. Letters are punched, struck, or exposed photographically onto a tape, and lines of words must then be pasted up. A photograph or film negative is made for the final label because headliners do not produce finished signs; that is, they can produce camera-ready copy, which then needs to be reproduced before the sign is complete. Headliners are slightly more complicated to use than press type, although

writing with type

Figure 43. This sample, made on a KroyType, shows proportional letter spacing. Both the headliner and the KroyType machines produce high-quality letters on a thin strip, ready for layouts.

they are faster. For large amounts of copy, the time and expense involved in operating a headliner may *not* make it preferable to typesetting.

Advantages of the headliner
• easy to operate;
• can select and use only the letters needed (there are no leftovers);
• choice of six typefaces.

Disadvantages of the headliner
• does not produce a finished sign;
• expense of tapes and disc may not be less than typesetting.
• relatively slow.

Figure 44. The inexpensive and versatile Leroy provides letters on paper, plastic, or wood in a one-step process.

Mechanical Lettering

For both clarity and economy, it is hard to beat the simple, mechanical hand lettering devices such as the Leroy letterer (figure 44). With proper attention to spacing, mechanical lettering can be made reasonably attractive and very legible. With a little practice, lettering can be done on many different surfaces, such as wood, paper, or plastic (see figure 45). Aside from the initial purchase of materials (stylus and templates), and the time needed for

Figure 45. Leroy lettering combined with artwork on this large board will be suitable for outdoor use.

production, costs are very low. While the letters produced by this method are very legible, they are not always of suitable quality for photographic enlargement or silk screen.

Advantages of mechanical lettering
• easy to learn, easy to use;
• inexpensive;
• can print on rigid surfaces;
• control over letter spacing.

Disadvantages of mechanical lettering
• limited choice of typefaces (only two are both legible and easy to make);
• letters are not of precision quality;
• it is difficult to correct mistakes.

The Typewriter

Despite the drawbacks, many labels are made with typewriters. Normal type, however, is too small for museum labels. If larger-than-normal type sizes are not available, typed labels can be photographically enlarged to the appropriate size. An enlargement formula is provided in the section "Type Sizes" in chapter 3.

Large type is produced with "primary school" typewriters, with IBM's Orator or Presentor typing elements, or on the IBM Executive, which offers proportional spacing.

Avoid typing in all capital letters. The "Orator" provides capitals in two sizes which are reasonably legible when used in combination.

When you are using typed characters of a normal size that will be enlarged, single space between the lines. If you are typing with the Orator, use a space and a half.

Because typed letters enlarged more than 200 percent lose resolution (figure 46), for greater enlargements it is better to start with press type or to have display type set professionally.

There are a few cases where original, typewritten labels in large type can be used suitably:

1. when exhibits are sure to change before the label fades;
2. if the exhibit is not crowded and every visitor has a good chance to get close to the label;
3. where labels are changed frequently to update the exhibit.

Advantages of typewritten labels
• they are cheap and quick.

Disadvantages of typewritten labels
• they have a quick, cheap look;
• letter spacing is not proportional on most typewriters;
• few choices of typefaces (only one is available in large type);
• photo enlargements further distort spacing.

writing

Figure 46. A 500 percent enlargement of normal typewriter type. Notice how the edges of the letters have changed.

Production Steps

One Step: Using Your Original

Hand lettered, typed, die-cut, engraved, proof-printed, mechanical, and dry-transfer lettering can all be used as originals. In some cases, the printed surface alone may be stiff enough to be placed on exhibit. Paper usually needs to be mounted on a more rigid surface. If anything happens to the original on display, you have to start again from scratch. If starting over is no big problem, use originals. If replacement is frequently necessary, you may want to use a copy for display.

Two Steps: Making A Copy

Most methods of lettering lend themselves to photographic reproduction. A photostat, or similar print, is a relatively inexpensive way of protecting your original that permits you to change the overall dimensions (enlarging or reducing) of the label for display. Most photostats are not stable, however, and will discolor in time. Extra washing and lamination will extend their life span considerably, but not enough for permanent (five to fifty years) exhibits. Photocopying black-and-white labels onto colored paper stock can enhance labels cheaply.

Several Steps

Copy is often typeset as a prerequisite to more elaborate production methods that involve photography (see figure 47).

Typeset copy→ Film negative→Film positive→ Silk screen
Scotchcal
Metal photo

A detailed discussion of the silk-screening process, plus directions on setting up an in-house, inexpensive system can be found in *Setting Up a Silk-Screening Facility* by Jean DuVal Kane.

Very briefly, the production of high-quality labels by silk screening involves:

1. producing original copy and art, usually black on white;
2. making a film negative and a film positive;

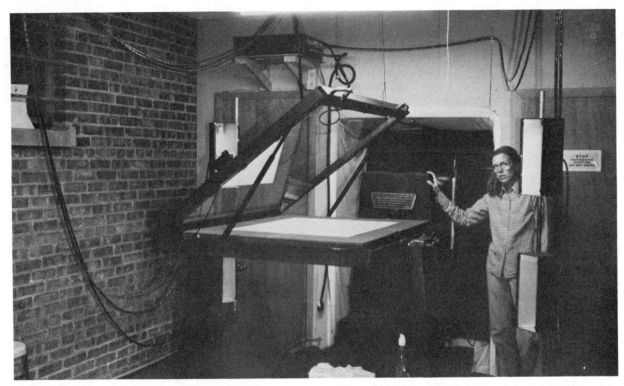

Figure 47. This process camera makes negatives as large as thirty-one square inches, large enough for most museum silk-screening jobs. Such negatives are also used for Scotchcal and metal photo production of labels.

3. placing the positive and prepared screen together and exposing to light;
4. washing out the unexposed portions of the screen, leaving a stencil;
5. applying ink to desired surface by forcing it through the screen.

One of the big advantages of silk screening is that it can be done on any flat surface, thus eliminating the need to place additional materials (other than the letters) on the background. (While it is considered very fashionable today to use white silk-screened letters against dark, colored backgrounds, white lettering in body copy on a dark ground is less legible than dark letters against light backgrounds.)

Silk-screened letters on the back of clear Plexiglas result in attractive, durable, protected copy. This process is referred to as subsurface printing. If it is improperly mounted, however, the copy will cast a shadow, giving the undesirable effect of a double image. By silk screening directly onto the matting of matted photographs (or prints), the labels will be attractive and safe since they will be out of reach inside the frames (see figure 48).

Another multistep production method with appeal for museums is Scotchcal, a photosensitive, adhesive-backed paper. The steps are similar to silk screening, but plastic or metal-colored paper is used rather than ink and screen. The steps are:

Interior of Field Columbian Museum, 1894

Crammed full of cases, the halls contained art, history, anthropology, agriculture, science, and technology. Later the scope of the collections was limited to four disciplines (anthropology, botany, geology, and zoology), and the depth of each increased from numerous expeditions around the world.

As the collections grew, however, the building deteriorated. The Palace of Fine Arts, like the other Exposition buildings, was meant to be temporary. Modifications to its structure allowed occupation for an unexpected 26 years, although the museum's trustees always planned for another, more permanent site.

Figure 48. This caption was silk screened in dark brown ink directly on the gray mat using Times Roman type (20 point on 23 point line spacing, ragged right).

1. prepare the original;
2. make a film negative;
3. expose Scotchcal paper and the film negative to ultraviolet light (a lightbox or even sunlight will do);
4. wash away unexposed areas with the solution provided by the manufacturer (basically alcohol);
5. peel off the backing, revealing the adhesive, and apply to a smooth surface.

Cleanup after this very simple process is easy, and Scotchcal involves little equipment or space and does not use any noxious chemicals requiring hooded ventilation systems. It is not cheap but is less expensive than out-of-house silk screening.

The steps for metal photo are similar to Scotchcal but are more involved and costly. The results, however, are extremely durable and are recommended for outdoor settings.

Placement

A few basic rules about placement will greatly contribute to the success of your labels and may be summarized briefly.

Don'ts
Don't stick labels on objects as if they were price tags (see figure 49).

Don't print body copy over photographs.

Don't put objects on top of labels.

Do's
Place labels at a 90-degree angle to the reader's line of vision. Tilt low labels back, high labels forward, and side labels out (see figures 50 and 51).

Locate labels as close as possible to the objects they describe.

When you use a code or number system to identify objects, put the label with the key close to the objects (figure 52).

Position labels of similar functions (for example, IDs, captions) consistently—always to the right, for example, or always below the object.

Situate labels so that there are no obstructions in the reader's line of vision. This rule is especially important if the label is in the rear of the case.

Mounting

The surest way to protect labels from the wear and tear of picking fingers is to mount them out of reach, but it is not always possible to do so. A good rule of thumb for signs mounted within reach is: if people cannot see what is holding it in place, they are less likely to fool with it.

Figure 49. Labels placed like price tags on paintings are not very attractive.

Figure 50. Labels placed very low necessitate the proverbial "prayer rug" reading position.

Figure 51. Long, angled railing provides a good reading surface, as does the eye-level stanchion (near left wall). ID labels near the floor (lower right) need larger lettering and should remain short.

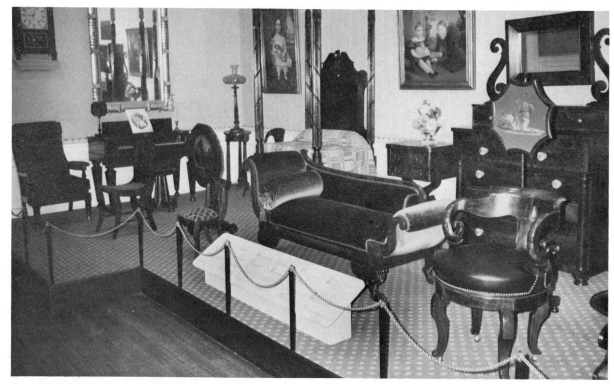

Figure 52. One label that is easy to find and to read uses line drawings that key objects to information.

Screws, tacks, and tape within view tempt idle fingers. In indoor situations where there is little temperature fluctuation and mounting is to be permanent, vinyl tape with double-sided adhesive, "hot glue," and silicone work well. For temporary mounting, double-sided tape, small screws, brackets, frames, Velcro tape, and Double-Lock tape are alternatives. Self-adhesive tape for use out of doors should be reinforced with stronger glue, such as epoxy.

Mounting often poses a unique problem: labels may need to be mounted "permanently" in terms of the visitors but may need to be easily changed by the museum staff when exhibits change. This dual requirement is especially true for seasonal outdoor exhibits and zoos (figures 53 and 54). Fasteners designed to meet such special needs are not yet fully developed. The stanchion-and-frame system is a costly solution; screws are unsightly; and glue is too permanent. Unfortunately, no cheap and easy solutions seem presently available. If you discover one, please let me know for future editions.

Figure 53. Outdoor label in a shaded location doubles as a locked box for the storage of touchable items.

Figure 54. The label on the front of the door conceals a box to which the tour leader holds the key. On the door's back is a visual aid (map), and inside are objects that visitors may touch.

6

Three Museums, Three Approaches

Each museum solves the problems of labeling in different ways. While the three cases described below are fictional, they contain many of the elements of real situations (see Serrell, "A Plan for Writing Interpretive Signs," and Rudin, "A Sign for All Seasons"). They exemplify a variety of ideal conditions—things worth striving for—in small, medium-sized, and large institutions. In each case, making museum labels is one part of the larger project of making museum exhibits, and labels are treated as integral to the total design, not as an afterthought. Labels are used as a means of interpretation rather than as mere identification, and they play an important educational role for each museum.

The different types of labels can be found in any type of museum. The subject matter will vary; the number of labels will vary, but the purposes and processes are likely to be similar. Labels mediate between object and visitor—whether the object is a painting, a photograph, an ancient jug, or a live animal—providing the stimulus to look more closely. Good labels increase visitors' observation power. During planning and throughout the label production schedule, all elements of the effective label should be given consideration: its function; the research necessary for content; the writing and editing; testing for effectiveness; and design and production. The order of these events will vary, as will the staff involved, depending on each museum's capabilities and resources.

A Small Historical Museum

This museum's director-curator-janitor is the only full-time staff, but on weekends several volunteers assist her. She writes all of the labels. She has studied the techniques of effective label writing, and brevity, clarity, and humor are evident in her efforts. Her friend and neighbor is a retired newspaper editor. He offered to help her edit the labels. Even though she understands the principles of good writing, she appreciates what an editor's objective skills can do. After the editor's reading, the labels are concise, sentences flow, and fuzzy thoughts have been sharpened.

On Saturdays a volunteer with secretarial experience helps type the labels and marks them for the typesetter. The town has three typesetting services, and the museum director has talked with all of them and has compared prices. She worked out a special rate with one company—

its president is a local history buff and wants to see the museum succeed. The typeset labels are pasted up by a second volunteer into a well-designed layout, and a volunteer photographer makes photostats of the copy, then dry mounts the labels onto mat board and bevels the edges for an attractive, finished look.

Some small exhibits need only a few labels. In such cases the director and the volunteers use twenty-four-point dry-transfer lettering for the larger labels and the Orator element on a borrowed IBM Selectric typewriter for the smaller captions and identification labels. Not counting time, this label budget is less than $500 a year.

A Medium-Sized Municipal Zoo

This small, old municipal facility has a very active zoo society. It successfully solicited money from local businesses to pay for a new master plan, part of which would place new emphasis on educational graphics throughout the zoo.

Because the zoo had a very small, overworked staff and all volunteers were already involved in other projects, the society hired a consultant to plan and implement the new sign program. The consultant designed a system that met three main objectives:

1. It would complement the existing strong education programs.

2. The system could be maintained or modified inexpensively as the zoo grew within its master plan.
3. It would give a new look to the old zoo and would offer positive evidence that the zoo was changing.

During a period of four months, the consultant conferred with keepers and other zoo staff, observed and interviewed zoo visitors (with the help of some volunteers), researched and wrote the label copy for all the new signs, met with the label committee for approval at different stages, designed the labels and had them set in type, produced the labels using Scotchcal, and installed them in time for the summer crowds.

The outdoor labels are expected to last about three years, during which time the parks department will begin to silk-screen more permanent signs on stock aluminum sign "blanks"—using the photonegatives that have already been processed for the Scotchcal labels. The cost of the new label program, including the consultant's time and all materials, was roughly $12,000.

A Large Museum of Natural History

Every new exhibit at this museum has an exhibit team assigned to it. A subject-matter expert (usually an in-house curator), a designer, and a person from the education department work together to make each exhibit a success.

The geology curator headed the team responsible for

renovating the museum's dinosaur hall. It was a massive job. The dinosaur hall, one of the largest and most popular exhibits, had vast quantities of label copy which needed updating and revising for the museum's younger audiences. (A visitor survey had revealed that the dinosaur hall was viewed by significantly more children five to sixteen years of age than any other major hall in the museum.) The curator was very skilled in his knowledge of the facts to be presented but needed to work with the educator to translate his thoughts into language appropriate for the average visitor. The educator also obtained valuable advice from the museum instructors, who spent many class sessions in the hall. Together they worked on the exhibit script and then passed it on to the museum editor, who reviewed and revised it according to the museum's own editorial style—developed over the years in the course of exhibit evaluations. After editing, the script was approved by the division director and was given to the designer.

The number of labels, the kinds of labels, and their general content were all decided ahead of time by the exhibit team. When the script had been edited, the designer presented several alternative layouts to the team. After some discussion, the team arrived at a decision (by consensus) favoring one design with some modifications. Label copy was typeset, according to the designer's specifications, by an in-house keyboard operator using the museum's new phototypesetter. All of the labels were silk-screened in the final exhibit production, after mock-ups had been tested with weekend family visitors and visiting sixth graders in school group programs. The label budget for the renovated hall, including staff time, was approximately $150,000.

These three cases have in common the following:
1. The person responsible for the writing had good communications skills.
2. The labels were well edited.
3. Pretesting with the intended audience was part of the total process.

The cases differ in the materials that were used to produce the labels—the choices made were determined chiefly by the money available. In all three museums, however, effective labels resulted.

Whatever your budget, by setting aside a little time and by planning thoughtfully, you too can create attractive, informative labels. Although this book has recommended guidelines for writing and production and sources of further information, it should be apparent that the process is creative, yielding results that can be as personally rewarding as they are effective in serving their purpose. Careful preparation of labels will increase your understanding of visitors to your museum. In addition, it will add to visitors' appreciation and enjoyment of your exhibits. Surely this is a large return for the effort spent.

Appendix: Resources

All of the companies listed make their catalogs available upon request (some charge a fee).

SUPPLIERS
Large letters for outdoor or indoor use

Plastic and foam
Ad-Mart
3480 Fulton Street
Brooklyn, NY 11208

Vinyl die cut
Zipatone, Inc.
150 Fencl Lane
Hillside, IL 60162

Die-cut machine
PST
Industrial Center Bldg.
Sausalito, CA 94965

Wood
Northland Products
Star Route 32
Rockland, ME 04841

Aluminum and bronze
Andco
4615 Sellars Avenue
P.O. Box 7366
Greensboro, NC 27407

Prespaced die-cut words
Letter-Rite Inc.
8219 W. Irving Park Road
Chicago, IL 60634

Plexiglas
Scott Plastics
P.O. Box 2958
Sarasota, FL 33578

Mittenite (mainly for indoor use)
Mitten Designer Letters
85 Fifth Avenue
New York, NY 10003

Large and small letters for indoor use
Dry transfer
Letraset USA, Inc.
40 Eisenhower Drive
Paramus, NJ 07652

Transfertech
1100 S. Kostner Avenue
Chicago, IL 60624

Cut out, self-adhesive, repositionable
Formatt
Graphic Products Corporation
Rolling Meadows, IL 60008

Mounting adhesives

Scott Plastics
P.O. Box 2958
Sarasota, FL 33578

Art materials
Brushes, Books, Frames, Glue, Paint, Ink, Furniture, etc.

Dick Blick Company
Knoxville Road
Galesburg, IL 61401

Mechanical lettering devices and machines

Leroy
Keuffel and Esser Company
309 Era Drive
Northbrook, IL 60062

Appendix: Resources

A. M. Varityper
11 Mount Pleasant Avenue
East Hanover, NJ 07936

KroyType
Kroy Industries
1728 Gervais Avenue
St. Paul, MN 55109

Engravograph
Hermes Plastics Midwest, Inc.
3642 128th Place
Alsip, IL 60658

Line-O-Scribe
Morgan Sign Press
4510 No. Ravenswood
Chicago, IL 60640

Typesetting

Check the Yellow Pages under "Photocopying and Typesetting."

Finished signs for indoor and outdoor use

Metal photo
Debien Marking Products Incorporated
3037 Lown Street North
St. Petersburg, FL 33713

Silk Screen
Modern Graphic Systems Inc.
4922 So. Western Ave.
Chicago, IL 60609

Scotchcal
B. Serrell and Associates
22649 Sherman Road
Chicago Heights, IL 60411

WHERE TO LEARN MORE

Several organizations offer workshops and seminars and will send brochures and schedules on request.

Office of Museum Programs
Smithsonian Institution
900 Jefferson Drive, Room 2235
Washington, DC 20560

Beverly Serrell and Associates
22649 Sherman Road
Chicago Heights, IL 60411

Exhibit Communication
   Research, Inc.
P.O. Box 11465
Shorewood, WI 53211

American Association for
   State and Local History
708 Berry Road
Nashville, TN 37204

An independent study course called "Interpretation through Effective Labels" is available from the American Association for State and Local History at the address shown above. For additional resources, consult *The Official Museum Products and Services Directory,* available through the American Association of Museums, 1055 Thomas Jefferson Street NW, Washington, DC 20007.

Bibliography

Alderson, William T. *Marking and Correcting Copy for Your Printer*. Technical Leaflet 51. Nashville: American Association for State and Local History, 1969.

Biggs, John R. *Basic Typography*. New York: Watson-Guptill, 1968.

Bloch, Milton. "Labels, Legends and Legibility." *Museum News*, vol. 47, no. 3 (1968), pp. 13–17.

Borun, Minda, and Maryanne Miller. "To Label or Not to Label." *Museum News*, vol. 58, no. 4 (1980), pp. 64–67.

———. *What's in a Name? A Study of the Effectiveness of Explanatory Labels in a Science Museum*. Philadelphia: Franklin Institute, 1980.

Casterline, Gail. *Archives and Manuscripts: Exhibits*. Chicago: Society of American Archivists, 1980.

Dair, Carl. *Design with Type*. Toronto: University of Toronto Press, 1967.

Flesch, R. F. *How to Test Readability*. New York: Harper and Row, 1951.

Fruitman, Michael, and Linda DuBro. "Writing Effective Labels." *Museum News*, vol. 57, no. 3 (1979), pp. 57–61.

Gore, Gary. *Phototypesetting: Getting the Most for Your Money*. Technical Leaflet 103. Nashville: American Association for State and Local History, 1978.

Kane, Jean DuVal. *Setting Up a Silk-Screening Facility: Guidelines for the Small Museum*. Technical Leaflet 68. Nashville: American Association for State and Local History, 1973.

Kleper, M. *Everything You Always Wanted to Know about In-Plant Typesetting*. Compugraphic Corporation, 1977.

Lakota, Robert. "Techniques for Improving Exhibit Effectiveness." In *Communicating with the Museum Visitor: Guidelines for Planning*. Toronto: Royal Ontario Museum (1976), p. 245–79.

Lee, Marshall. *Bookmaking: The Illustrated Guide to Design/Production/Editing*. 2nd ed. New York: R. R. Bowker, 1979.

Loomis, Ross. "Please! Not Another Visitor Survey." *Museum News*, vol. 52, no. 2 (1973), pp. 21–26.

Loomis, Ross and Hummel, Carl F. "Observations and Recommendations on Visitor Utilization Problems and Potentials of the Denver Museum of Natural History." *Denver Museum of Natural History Working Papers in Visitor Studies*, no. 1 1975.

Lucas, Frederic A. "Museum Labels and Labeling." *Proceedings of the American Association of Museums*, vol. 5 (1911), pp. 91–101.

Neal, Arminta. "Labels." In *Exhibits for the Small Museum*. Nashville: American Association for State and Local History, 1976.

North, F. J. "Notes for Students: Labels: Their Function, Preparation and Use." *Museums Journal*, vol. 49, nos. 2, 3, and 4 (1949), pp. 26–30, 55–62, 80–86.

Paterson, D. G., and M. A. Tinker. *How to Make Type Readable*. New York: Harper and Row, 1940.

Pocket Pal: A Graphic Arts Production Handbook. 12th ed. New York: International Paper Company, 1979.

Prince, J. H. "Printing for the Visually Handicapped." *Journal of Typographical Research*, vol. 1 (1967), p. 31.

Rabb, George. "The Unicorn Experiment." *Curator*, vol. 12, no. 4 (1969), pp. 257–62.

———. "Signs—Essential Link with the Public." *American Association of Zoological Parks and Aquariums Annual Conference Proceedings*, (1975), pp. 140–3.

Rudin, Emily. "A Sign for All Seasons." *Curator*, vol. 22, no. 4 (1979), pp. 303–9.

Screven, Chandler. *The Measurement and Facilitation of Learning in the Museum Environment: An Experimental Analysis*. Washington, D.C.: Smithsonian Institution Press, 1974.

Bibliography

————. "Visitor Attention and Learning in Public Exhibits and the Role of Evaluation." *American Association of Zoological Parks and Aquariums Annual Conference Proceedings*, (1979), pp. 151–9.

Serrell, Beverly. "A Plan for Writing Interpretive Signs." *Curator*, vol. 22, no. 4 (1979), pp. 299–302.

————. "Looking at Visitors at Zoos and Aquariums." *Museum News*, vol. 59, no. 3 (1980), pp. 36–41.

Shettel, Harris. "Exhibits: Art Form or Educational Medium?" *Museum News*, vol. 52, no. 1 (1973), pp. 32–41.

Spencer, Herbert. *The Visible Word*. Visual Communication Books. New York: Hastings House, 1968.

Strunk, William, Jr., and E. B. White. *The Elements of Style*. 3rd ed. New York: Macmillan, 1979.

Tilden, Freeman. "The Written Word." In *Interpreting Our Heritage*. 3rd ed. Chapel Hill, N.C.: University of North Carolina Press, 1977.

Turnbull, A., and R. Baird. *The Graphics of Communication*. 4th ed. New York: Holt, Rinehart and Winston, 1980.

Turnbull, A. T., and D. E. Carter. "Readership of Advertising with All-Display Typography." *Visible Language*, vol. 2 (1971), p. 157.

Weiner, George. "Why Johnny Can't Read Labels." *Curator*, vol. 6, no. 2 (1963), pp. 143–56.

White, Jan. V. *Editing by Design*. New York: R. R. Bowker, 1974.

Wilson, Don, and Dennis Medina. *Exhibit Labels: A Consideration of Content*. Technical Leaflet 60. Nashville: American Association for State and Local History, 1972.

Witteborg, Lothar. *Good Show! A Practical Guide for Temporary Exhibitions*. Washington, D.C.: Smithsonian Institution, 1981.

Zinsser, William. *On Writing Well*. 2nd ed. New York: Harper and Row, 1980.

Index

Index

This book was set in the Mergenthaler version of Helvetica
in light and bold weights. It was printed in offset lithography
on Glatfelter paper.